English as a Second Language
Elementary Cycle Two

Grade **4**

Caroline Simard

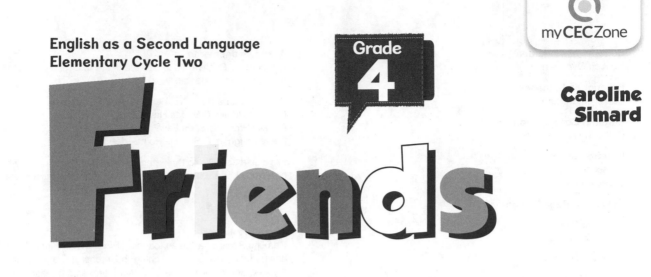

Friends

Learning and **Activities**

myCECZone

LES ÉDITIONS
CEC

9001, boul. Louis-H.-La Fontaine, Anjou (Québec) Canada H1J 2C
Téléphone : 514 351-6010 · Télécopieur : 514 351-3534

W9-AVY-151

Editorial Management
Colleen Ovenden

Production Management
Danielle Latendresse

Editorial Coordination
Katherine Akerley

Proofreading
Katherine Akerley
Josée Lafrenière

Cover and Page Design

accent
tonique

Ⓜ INTERSCRIPT

Illustrations
Laurence Dechassey

Les Éditions CEC inc. remercient le gouvernement du Québec de l'aide financière accordée à l'édition de cet ouvrage par l'entremise du Programme de crédit d'impôt pour l'édition de livres, administré par la SODEC.

Friends, Learning and Activities, **Grade 4**
Friends, Learning and Activities, **Grade 4**, Teacher's Copy

Dépôt légal : 2015
Bibliothèque et Archives nationales du Québec
Bibliothèque et Archives Canada

ISBN: 978-2-7617-7854-1 (Learning and Activities Book)
ISBN: 978-2-7617-7855-8 (Learning and Activities Book, version MaZone avec activités interactives, 1 an, livraison postale)
ISBN: 978-2-7617-8153-4 (Learning and Activities Book, version MaZone avec activités interactives, 1 an livraison numérique)
ISBN: 978-2-7617-8392-7 (Teacher's Copy, avec CD)
ISBN: 978-2-7617-8393-4 (Teacher's Copy, version MaZone pour 1 an, livraison numérique)
ISBN: 978-2-7617-8394-1 (Teacher's Copy, version MaZone pour 5 ans, livraison numérique)

Imprimé au Canada
3   4   5   6   7   23   22   21   20   19

Acknowledgements
Les Éditions CEC would like to thank the following consultants for their valuable feedback:

Sophie Charpentier, C.S. des Grandes-Seigneuries
Caroline Poulin, C.S. des Navigateurs
Rosalie Proce, C.S. de Laval
Pierre St-Ignan, C.S. de la Pointe-de-l'Île

We would also like to thank the focus group participants who helped us better understand and respond to the realities of today's ESL classroom.

About the author
Caroline Simard has been teaching ESL for 13 years in Lévis and has had the pleasure of teaching the intensive program for the last 8 years. Before joining the CEC team, first as a pedagogical consultant and then as an author, she worked with the MELS on several projects and was part of ESL communities at her school board. The author firmly believes that student teamwork and cooperation are at the base of ESL learning and has tried her best to make sure that these are the underlying values throughout this book.

Author acknowledgements
The author wishes to thank Les Éditions CEC for the opportunity to write this book and to reach one of her career goals. The realization of this book would not have been possible without Colleen Ovenden's structured mind, humorous comments, professionalism and continuous support, and Patrick Johnston's input and kindness. The author also wishes to thank Katherine Akerley for her patience, attention to detail, and positive and encouraging feedback. Finally, the author would like to thank Philippe, Clara and Rosemarie for their sacrifices, understanding and ongoing support throughout this journey.

This book is dedicated to Elisabeth Vatcher, the ESL teacher who inspired the author to become an ESL teacher, and to Wendy Williams, who inspired the author to become an author. Thank you, Wendy, for everything.

Audio CD Credits
All flawless audio programming and mixing provided by Pierre Laurendeau from Les Productions IMMM. www.immm.ca

Special thanks to Jaren Cerf for her artistic collaboration and allowing us to use her spectacular voice in all of our songs. www.jarencerf.com

FSC
www.fsc.org
MIXTE
Papier issu
de sources
responsables
FSC® C011825

Table of Contents

Welcome to Friends, Grade 4

I'm Leo, and these are my friends! Follow us in *Friends, Grade 4.*

Hi, I am Eddie. I like castles.

Hi, I am Ariane. I like art!

Hi, I am Lexie. I like hockey!

Hi, I am Robin. I like music.

Units

There are seven units in *Friends, Grade 4.*

Pre-unit

► **Prepare** for Grade 4 with activities in the Pre-unit.

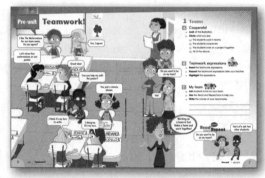

Units 1 to 6

► **Start** a unit with an **exploration of the vocabulary** for the theme and an oral interaction activity.

► **Do the oral interaction**

Practise your oral interaction right away!

► **Read the dialogue**

Start each unit with an important question or idea.

► *Look at Words*

Use the word lists for the Illustration or an activity.

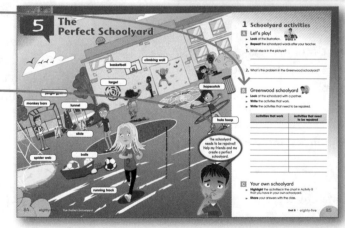

L👀k at Words

Actions	catch	climb	jump	play	run	throw
Activities	balls	running track	basketball	target		
	climbing wall	hopscotch				

► *Read and Review*

Review previously learned grammar notions.

Read and Review

- Singular noun + **is**
  The ball **is** in the basketball net.
- Plural noun + **are**
  The balls **are** in the basket.

► **Continue** in the unit with oral interaction, grammar practice, games and also read-along stories, songs and other listening activities.

► *Stop and Think*

Self-monitor your use of strategies in a section of a unit.

STOP and Think

I speak English. ◯   I cooperate. ◯   I ask for help or clarification. ◯

► *Read and Repeat*

Pay attention to this model for any oral task.

Read and Repeat

Can you run? — Yes, I can! — Can you climb? — No, I can't.

► *Look at Grammar*

Learn the grammar notions to help with writing. Do interactive activities on the My CEC Zone platform.

My CEC ZONE

Look at Grammar: Capabilities

We use *can* to talk about capability.

Question	Affirmative	Negative
Can you catch?	Yes, I **can**.	No, I **cannot**. / No, I **can't**.
Can she jump?	Yes, she **can**.	No, she **cannot**. / No, she **can't**.
Can he throw?	Yes, he **can**.	No, he **cannot**. / No, he **can't**.

► *Story time*

Read along with the audio in the Teacher's Copy or on the My CEC Zone platform.

► *Link It Together* and the *Project* pages

Review the unit and get ready for the final project.

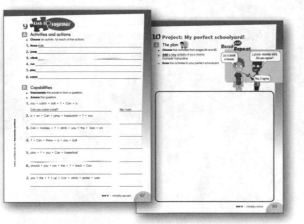

Resources

Review this section for help in all activities.

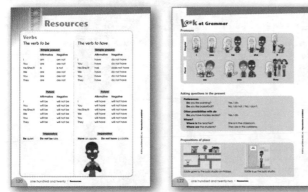

1 Teams

A Cooperate!

► **Look** at the illustration.

► **Circle** what you see.

   a) The students work in teams.

   b) The students cooperate.

   c) The students work on a project together.

   d) All of the above.

B Teamwork expressions

► **Read** the teamwork expressions.

► **Repeat** the teamwork expressions after your teacher.

► **Highlight** the expressions.

C My team

► **Ask** students to be on your team.

► **Use** the *Read and Repeat* box to help you.

► **Write** the names of your teammates.

_____

_____

Do you want to be on my team?

Yes!

Working as a team is fun! Make a team and work together!

Read and **Repeat**

Do you want to be on my team?

Yes! Let's ask two other students.

2 Team talk

A Act it out

► **Mime** a teamwork expression from pages 6 and 7.

► **Take turns** guessing the expression.

B Great idea!

► **Read** the clues to your teammates, using the cards your teacher gives you.

► **Decide** which teamwork expression to use.

► **Write** the teamwork expression on the line.

Read and Repeat

I think it's "Just a minute, please." Do you agree?

Yes, I agree!

1. _____

2. _____

3. _____

4. _____

5. _____

6. _____

7. _____

8. _____

9. _____

10. _____

C Team castle

► **Use** the cards from Activity B to make your team castle.

► **Place** each card one at a time.

► **Say** the expression for the situation on the card.

► **Be** the first team to finish your castle and **win** the class competition!

3 Pronouns

Lk at Grammar: Pronouns

We use pronouns to replace nouns.

Singular

| I | you | he | she | it |

Plural

we   you   they

A   We cooperate

► **Highlight** the correct pronoun in the second sentence.

1. Hi! My name is <u>Lexie</u>. **I / We** work in a team.

2. <u>My classmates and I</u> work on projects. **We / They** think it is important to cooperate.

3. <u>Robin</u> is a good team member. **I / He** listens to his teammates' ideas.

4. <u>Ariane</u> is polite. **I / She** waits her turn to speak.

5. <u>Eddie</u> helps everybody! **She / He** asks, "Can I help you?"

6. <u>Ariane and Robin</u> encourage their team. **They / We** say, "Great idea!"

7. <u>I</u> am very creative. **I / You** share my ideas.

8. <u>Eddie, Ariane and I</u> are in English class. **They / We** love to participate in team projects!

9. <u>You</u> work in teams. Do **I / you** cooperate?

STOP and Think

I cooperate.   I speak English.   I use what I know.

B The pronoun song

► **Listen** to the song.

► **Write** the pronouns that are missing.

These are pronouns you can learn. Let's sing them all together.

I, you, he, she, _____. I, you, _____, she, it. I, _____, he, _____, it. _____, you, _____.

4 Teamwork skills

L∞k at Grammar: The verb *to be*

We use the verb *to be* to talk about ourselves or others.

Singular	Plural
I **am**	We **are**
You **are**	You **are**
He/She/It **is**	They **are**
I **am** in Grade 4.	We **are** at school.
He **is** 10 years old.	They **are** helpful.

A I agree!

► **Read** the definitions.

► **Repeat** the teamwork skills after your teacher.

L∞k at Words: Teamwork skills

attentive: looking at and listening to teammates when they speak

helpful: ready to give assistance

collaborative: able to share ideas, to work with teammates

patient: able to wait politely

supportive: encouraging and understanding

cooperative: all of the above!

B Am, is, are

► **Write** the correct form of the verb *to be*.

► **Use** the *Look at Grammar* box on page 10 to help you.

1. She ___is___ supportive.

2. They _____ attentive.

3. We _____ patient.

4. He _____ collaborative.

5. I _____ helpful.

6. You _____ cooperative.

C Team players

► **Replace** the noun with a pronoun.

► **Write** the correct form of the verb *to be*.

► **Write** the teamwork skill that matches the description.

Pronoun	Verb *to be*	Teamwork skill

1. **Robin** listens to his teammates' ideas.

| He | is | attentive. |

2. **Ariane** waits her turn to speak.

3. **Eddie** assists everybody.

4. **Ariane and Robin** encourage their teammates.

5. **I** share my ideas.

6. **Robin, Eddie, Ariane and I** cooperate!

D Are you cooperative?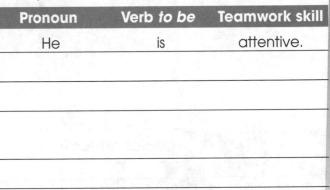

Step 1

► **Look** at the teamwork skills in the *Look at Words* box on page 10.

► **Highlight** the teamwork skills that correspond to you.

Step 2

► **Share** your teamwork skills with your teammates.

► **Complete** the hand on the sheet your teacher gives you.

► **Look** at the model to help you.

> I am helpful.

> I am supportive.

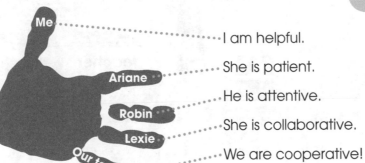

Me ········· I am helpful.

Ariane ······· She is patient.

Robin ····· He is attentive.

Lexie ···· She is collaborative.

Our team ····· We are cooperative!

1 New Faces, New Places

principal

secretary

special educator

lunch monitor

nurse

L☺ok at Grammar: The verb *to be*

We use the verb *to be* to talk about ourselves or others.

Singular	Plural
I **am**	We **are**
You **are**	You **are**
He / She / It **is**	They **are**
I **am** in Grade 4.	We **are** at school.
He **is** 10 years old.	They **are** helpful.

teacher

librarian

janitor

1 Occupations: School people

A Who is who?

► **Look** at the illustration.

► **Repeat** the occupation words after your teacher.

B People in your school

► **Read** the questions.

► **Write** the name of each person in your school.

1. What is the name of the janitor?

_____

2. What is the name of the principal?

_____

3. What is the name of one teacher?

_____

4. What is the name of one lunch monitor?

_____

5. What is the name of the librarian?

_____

6. What is the name of the secretary?

_____

7. What is the name of the special educator?

_____

8. What is the name of the nurse?

_____

Hello! I am Leo!
I am a new student at
Greenwood School.
Help me get to know
school people
and places!

2 New faces

A New names

► **Take turns** reading the clues on the cards your teacher gives you.

► **Write** the person's occupation.

► **Draw** a line to the person's face.

1. Mr. Fisher is the <u>janitor</u>_____.

2. Ms. Johnson is the _____.

3. Mr. Esposito is the _____.

4. Ms. Chan is the _____.

5. Ms. Elisabeth is a _____.

6. Mr. O'Dell is the _____.

7. Ms. Gloria is the _____.

8. Mr. Pierre is a _____.

B Principal's message

► **Listen** to the message.

► **Write** the occupations.

► **Use** the occupation words on pages 12 and 13 to help you.

1. _____ **4.** _____ **7.** _____

2. _____ **5.** _____ **8.** _____

3. _____ **6.** _____

3 Who does what?

A Occupation actions

▶ **Repeat** the occupation actions after your teacher.

Look at Words: Occupation actions

meet

answer

teach

organize

care for

clean

place

help

B Who am I?

▶ **Write** the correct occupations and occupation actions.

1. I am the _____librarian_____ . I _____place_____ books on shelves.

2. I am the _____ . I _____ the floor.

3. I am the _____ . I _____ the tables at lunch.

4. I am the _____ . I _____ parents.

5. I am the _____ . I _____ students with conflicts.

6. I am the _____ . I _____ sick students.

7. I am the _____ . I _____ the phone.

8. I am a _____ . I _____ English.

C Charades

- ▶ **Play** charades with the occupation actions.
- ▶ **Take turns** guessing the occupation.

Read and Review

The verb *to be*:

I **am** the principal.

You **are** the librarian.

Read and Repeat

You clean the floor! You are the janitor.

Yes, I am!

4 The present

Look at Grammar: The present: third person singular

Add -**s** to most verbs for the third person singular.
Add -**es** when the verb ends with -*ch*.

Singular	**1st person**	I meet	I teach
	2nd person	You meet	You teach
	3rd person	He/She/It meet**s**	He/She/It teach**es**
Plural	**1st person**	We meet	We teach
	2nd person	You meet	You teach
	3rd person	They meet	They teach

A What does she do?

- ▶ **Read** the sentences.
- ▶ **Highlight** the correct answer.

1. She place / She places
2. It meets / It meet
3. He organizes / He organize
4. She teach / She teaches
5. It clean / It cleans
6. She helps / She help
7. He care for / He cares for
8. She answer / She answers

B School people in action

► **Read** the paragraphs with a partner.

► **Highlight** the occupation actions.

► **Add** -*s* or -*es* to the verbs in the third person singular.

Leo walk**s** around the school with Ms. Elisabeth. He see many staff members doing different things. The principal meet a parent. The secretary answer the phone. The librarian place books on shelves. The nurse care for a sick student.

They continue down the hallway. The lunch monitor organize the tables for lunch. The janitor clean the washroom. The special educator help students with a conflict. A teacher teach math. Finally, they arrive at Leo's classroom. All of the students say, "Hello Leo!"

C It's a match!

► **Match** the pronoun with the occupation action, using the cards your teacher gives you.

► **Remember** their place.

► **Collect** the most cards and **win** the game!

Read **and** Repeat

"She" and "answer**s** the phone." Do you agree?

Yes, I agree. It's a match. It's my turn.

STOP and Think

I take risks. ◯   I use resources. ◯   I cooperate. ◯

5 School places

A Where is everyone?

► **Repeat** after your teacher.

► **Answer** your teacher's questions.

L👀k at Grammar: Where?

We use *where + is* or *are* to ask about the location of a person.

Where is the teacher? She is in the classroom.

Where are the students? They are in the cafeteria.

L👀k at Words: School places

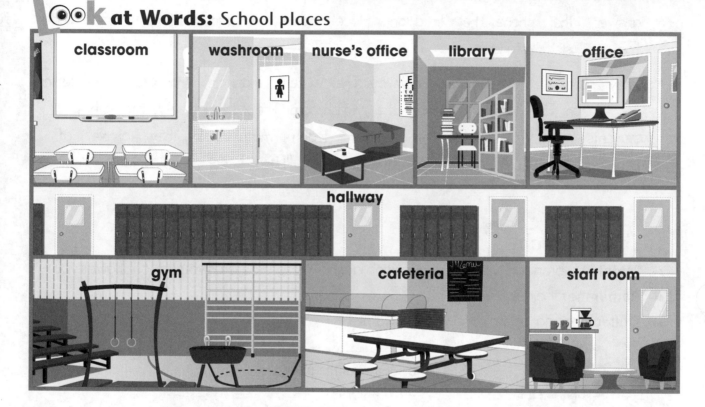

classroom washroom nurse's office library office

hallway

gym cafeteria staff room

B School people in school places

► **Read** the sentences.

► **Ask** where the school people are.

1. The janitor is in the washroom. Where is the janitor? _____

2. The teachers are in the classroom. _____

3. The nurse is in the nurse's office. _____

4. The librarian is in the library. _____

5. The principal is in the office. _____

6. The students are in the gym. _____

7. The special educator is in the hallway. _____

8. The lunch monitors are in the cafeteria. _____

C Blackout at Greenwood School

► **Use** the card your teacher gives you.

► **Ask** your classmates where the school people are.

► **Write** the school people in the correct flashlight spots.

Read and Repeat

Where is the janitor?

The janitor is in the nurse's office!

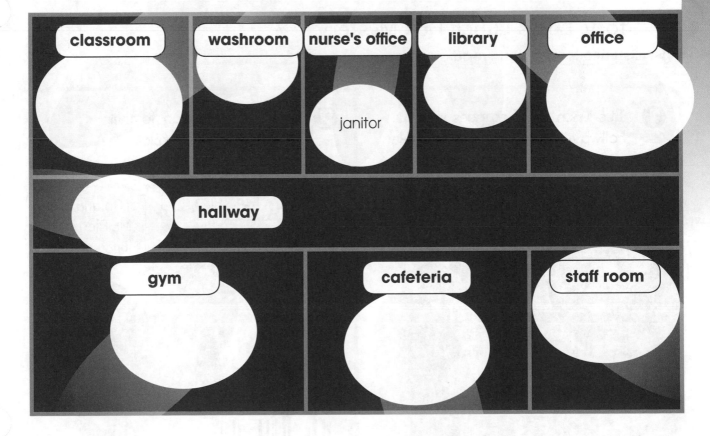

classroom	washroom	nurse's office	library	office
		janitor		

hallway

gym

cafeteria

staff room

6 Story time

A Prepare to read

▶ **Read** the title and **skim** the story.

▶ **Answer** the questions.

1. What is this story about? Circle the correct answer.
   a) Leo visits his new school.
   b) Leo looks for his lost lunch box.
   c) Leo is lost in his new school.

2. Name three school places in the story.

_____   _____

3. Who gives Leo his lunch box?

_____

_____

_____

L👀k at Words

lost: could not find something (the past tense of *lose*)

brought: came to a place with something (the past tense of *bring*)

B Story: Leo's Lunch Box Mystery

▶ **Listen** to the story and **read** along.

1 It's lunchtime! Leo goes into the hallway to get his lunch box. He can't find it.

What is wrong, Leo?

I can't find my lunch box! I think I **lost** it.

I can help you find it.

2 Leo and Ariane go to their classroom. They explain the problem to Ms. Elisabeth.

I am sorry, Leo. It is not in the classroom.

Go and ask Mr. Pierre, the lunch monitor.

7 It's lunchtime! Leo and his classmates go to the cafeteria to eat.

Do you like Greenwood School, Leo?

Yes! People are very nice. Ariane helped me find my lunch box.

That is what friends are for!

C Show you understand

► **Scan** the story to find the answers.

1. Who helps Leo look for his lunch box? Highlight the correct answer.
- the lunch monitor (Mr. Pierre), Ariane and Eddie
- the special educator (Ms. Gloria) and Lexie
- the principal (Mr. O'Dell) and Ariane

2. Where does Leo find his lunch box?

_____

3. Write the school places in the order the students go to them.

a) _____ b) _____ c) _____

d) _____ e) _____

4. Your turn
- ► **Choose** a school place that is *not* in the story.
- ► **Draw** a scene with Leo's lunch box.
- ► **Complete** the sentence in the box.

Leo finds his lunch box in the

_____

5. Do you forget things at home? If yes, what?

_____

STOP and Think

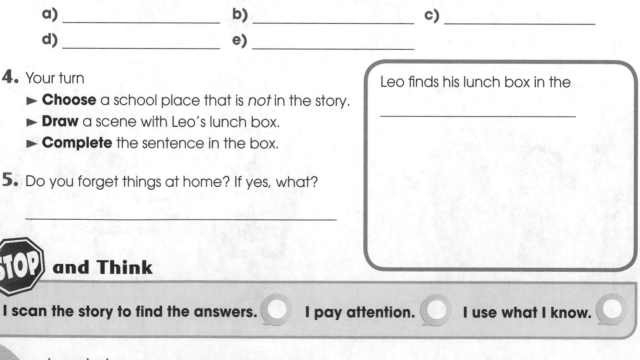

I scan the story to find the answers. ◯   I pay attention. ◯   I use what I know. ◯

7 People who help you

A Help!

▶ **Repeat** the vocabulary words after your teacher.

Look at Words: Things you need help with

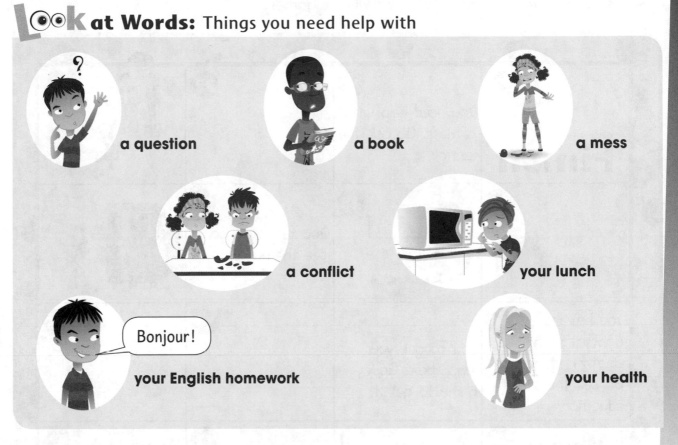

a question

a book

a mess

a conflict

your lunch

Bonjour!

your English homework

your health

B Problem? Solution!

▶ **Match** the problem with the correct solution, using the cards your teacher gives you.

Read and Repeat

"You need help with a book."
"Go see the nurse."

No, it's not
a match.

8 Learn and play

A Action, reaction

► **Follow** the instructions and **move** around the game.
► **Be** the first player to get to *Finish* and **win** the game!

24 **23** You need help with a mess. Go ask the janitor. **22** **21**

Finish

17 **18** **19** You feel sick. Go see the nurse. **20**

16 You have a conflict with another student. Go see the special educator. **15** You forget your lunch box. Go home to get it. **14** **13**

9 **10** **11** **12** You need help with your English homework. Go see the teacher.

8 You have questions about school. Go see the secretary or the principal. **7** **6** **5** It's time for lunch! Go to the cafeteria.

Start **1** Home **2** **3** You need help with a book. Go see the librarian. **4**

B Word search

► **Unscramble** the letters and write the school people, school places and occupation actions on the lines.

► **Find** the school words in the puzzle.

► **Write** the circled letters on the lines to find the mystery expression.

1. wrsaen   a(n)s w e r

2. iefcraate   _ _ _ _ _ _ _ _ _

3. rrcfaeo   _ _ _ (_) _ _ _

4. msaloscor   _ _ _ _ _ _ _ _ _

5. anelc   _ _ _ _ _

6. ymg   _ _ _

7. lyhlawa   _ _ _ _ (_) _

8. phle   _ _ _ _

9. itjraon   _ _ _ _ _ _ _

10. rrbiiaaln   _ _ _ _ _ _ _ _ _

11. aybrlir   _ _ _ _ _ _ _

12. uhlcn niormto   _ _ _ _ _   _ _ _ _ _ _ _

13. uesnr   _ _ _ _ _

14. cofefi   _ _ (_) _ _ _

15. iozegran   _ _ _ (_) _ _ _ _

16. plrnipiac   _ _ _ _ _ _ _ _ _

17. eecstyarr   _ _ (_) _ _ _ _ _ _

18. plecasi crodetau   _ _ _ _ _ _   _ _ _ _ _ _ _ _

19. fsatf omro   _ _ _ _ _   _ _ _ _

20. ehtac   _ (_) _ _ _

21. aerchet   _ _ _ _ _ _ _

22. hawmosor   _ _ (_) _ _ _ _ _

r	e	a	t	e	l	l	c	s	n	y	e
o	s	n	e	c	i	u	a	e	w	a	f
t	r	s	a	i	b	n	f	c	a	w	r
a	u	w	c	f	r	c	e	r	r	l	o
c	n	e	h	f	a	h	t	e	o	l	t
u	l	r	e	o	r	m	e	t	f	a	i
d	i	a	r	c	i	o	r	a	e	h	n
e	b	n	s	e	a	n	i	r	r	s	a
l	r	a	n	s	n	i	a	y	a	h	j
a	a	e	e	w	r	t	p	l	c	c	a
i	r	l	s	m	o	o	r	h	s	a	w
c	y	c	m	y	g	r	o	h	c	e	e
e	z	i	n	a	g	r	o	m	e	t	s
p	r	i	n	c	i	p	a	l	f	l	x
s	m	o	o	r	f	f	a	t	s	l	p

Mystery expression: N_ _ _ _   _ _ _ _ _ _

9 Link It Together

A Occupations

► **Look** at the illustrations.

► **Write** the occupations.

Example: <u>special educator</u>

1. _____ 2. _____ 3. _____ 4. _____

B Occupation actions

► **Read** the descriptions.

► **Circle** true or false.

1. The principal meets parents.	True	False
2. The librarian cares for sick students.	True	False
3. The janitor cleans the floor.	True	False
4. The secretary answers the phone and answers questions.	True	False
5. The nurse helps students with conflicts.	True	False
6. The special educator teaches English.	True	False

C Who does what at school?

► **Complete** the sentences with the correct action.

► **Write** the person's occupation.

1. She _____ helps _____ with conflicts.   the special educator _____

2. She _____ the phone.   _____

3. He _____ lunchtime.   _____

4. She _____ books on the shelves.   _____

5. She _____ English.   _____

D School places

► **Read** the questions.

► **Look** at the illustrations below.

► **Answer** the questions using full sentences.

1. Where is Leo? He is in the classroom.

2. Where is Lexie? _____

3. Where is Robin? _____

4. Where is Ariane? _____

5. Where is Eddie? _____

6. Where is Leo? _____

E Match it up!

► **Read** the words on the left.

► **Draw** a line to the correct place.

You need help with...	You go to the...
1. your English homework	library
2. your health	office
3. a conflict	nurse's office
4. your lunch	classroom
5. a mess	washroom
6. a book	hallway
7. a question	cafeteria

10 Project: A guide for a new student

A The plan

▶ **Choose** four things a new student needs help with.

▶ **Put** a check (✓) in the four boxes.

▶ **Match** the things a new student needs help with to the school people and the school places.

1. conflict ☐   **4.** health ☐   **7.** mess ☐

2. English homework ☐   **5.** questions ☐

3. lunch ☐   **6.** book ☐

Things a new student needs help with	School people	School places

B The model

▶ **Complete** the model with occupations, actions, places and the things students need help with.

You are new at Greenwood School. Let me help you, my friend!

Ms. Elisabeth is the _____ teacher _____ . She _____ teaches _____ English. She is in the _____ classroom _____ if you need help with your ___ English homework ___ .

Ms. Chan is the _____ . She _____ books on the shelves. She is in the _____ if you need help with a _____ .

Mr. Pierre is the _____ . He _____ lunchtime. He is in the _____ if you need help with your _____ .

Mr. Esposito is the _____ . He _____ sick students. He is in the _____ if you need help with your _____ .

C The rough draft

► **Use** your plan from Activity A and the model from Activity B to write a guide for your school.

_____

_____

_____

_____

_____

_____

_____

_____

_____

_____

D The presentation

► **Choose** five things you need help with.

► **Write** them in the chart.

► **Find** someone who can help you.

I need help with...	Classmate's name
a conflict	Robin
1.	
2.	
3.	
4.	
5.	

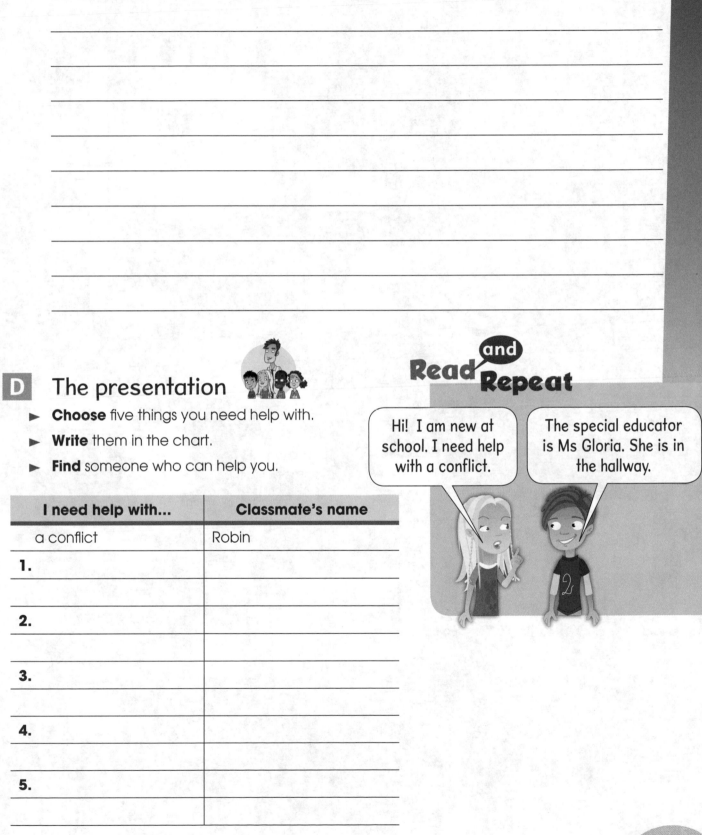

Read and Repeat

Hi! I am new at school. I need help with a conflict.

The special educator is Ms Gloria. She is in the hallway.

Monster Party Invitation

hair

nose

eye

mouth

head

arm

claws

tongue

hand

leg

tail

foot

orange Juice

1 Humans and monsters

A Party time!

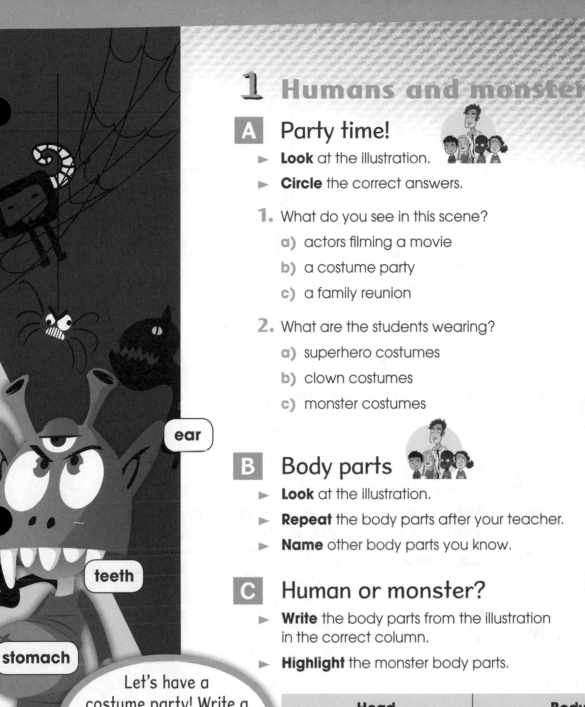

▶ **Look** at the illustration.

▶ **Circle** the correct answers.

1. What do you see in this scene?

　a) actors filming a movie

　b) a costume party

　c) a family reunion

2. What are the students wearing?

　a) superhero costumes

　b) clown costumes

　c) monster costumes

B Body parts

▶ **Look** at the illustration.

▶ **Repeat** the body parts after your teacher.

▶ **Name** other body parts you know.

C Human or monster?

▶ **Write** the body parts from the illustration in the correct column.

▶ **Highlight** the monster body parts.

ear

teeth

stomach

Let's have a costume party! Write a party invitation and describe your monster costume.

Head	Body
head	arm

2 Body chants

A Busy head

► **Practise** the chant with your teacher.

► **Point** to the parts of your head as you sing.

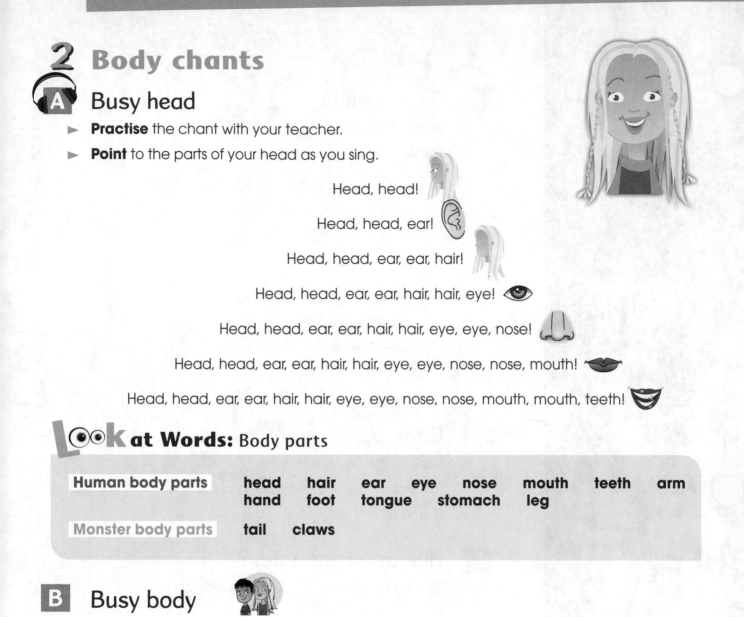

Head, head!

Head, head, ear!

Head, head, ear, ear, hair!

Head, head, ear, ear, hair, hair, eye!

Head, head, ear, ear, hair, hair, eye, eye, nose!

Head, head, ear, ear, hair, hair, eye, eye, nose, nose, mouth!

Head, head, ear, ear, hair, hair, eye, eye, nose, nose, mouth, mouth, teeth!

L👀k at Words: Body parts

Human body parts	head	hair	ear	eye	nose	mouth	teeth	arm
	hand	foot	tongue	stomach	leg			
Monster body parts	tail	claws						

B Busy body

► **Create** your own chant.

► **Use** <u>five</u> **human** body parts and <u>two</u> **monster** body parts.

► **Look** at Activity A to help you.

_____

_____

_____

_____

_____

_____

3 Body descriptions

L👀k at Grammar: Adjectives

We use an adjective to describe a noun. We place adjectives before the noun.

one small nose   **one big** nose   **two pointy** ears   **two round** ears

dark hair   **light** hair   **green** eyes   **three short** tails   **three long** tails

A Body part descriptions

► **Look** at the cards your teacher gives you.

► **Write** a description of the body parts on each card.

► **Include** numbers with the body parts.

► **Use** the *Look at Words* box to help you.

L👀k at Words

Singular	Plural
tooth	teeth
foot	feet
hair	hair

1. two pointy teeth _____

2. _____

3. _____

4. _____

5. _____

6. _____

7. _____

8. _____

9. _____

10. _____

11. _____

12. _____

B The missing body part

► **Place** the cards from Activity A on page 33 on your desk.

► **Ask** your teammates to close their eyes.

► **Remove** one card.

► **Ask** your teammates to say which card is missing.

Read and Repeat

Which card is missing?

I think "two pointy teeth" is missing.

C Choose and draw

► **Draw** a monster with five body parts from Activity A on page 33.

► **Write** the body parts.

► **Compare** your drawing with your teammates' drawings.

STOP and Think

I speak English. ◯   I cooperate. ◯   I ask for help or clarification. ◯

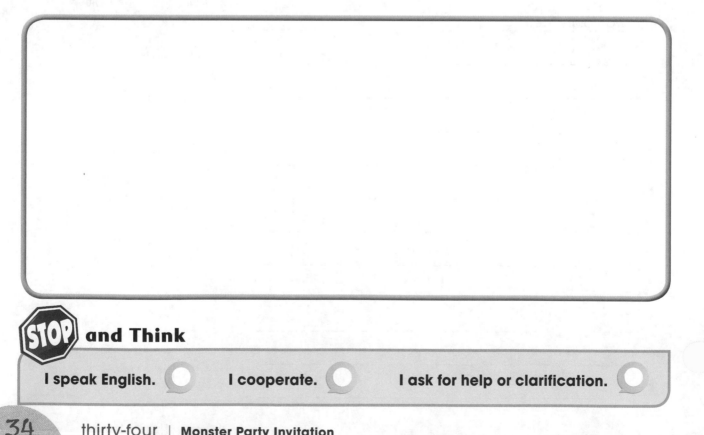

4 I have, you have

L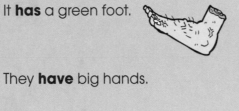k at Grammar: The verb *to have*

We use the verb *to have* to talk about possession.

Singular	I **have**	It **has** a green foot.
	You **have**	
	He/She/It **has**	
Plural	We **have**	They **have** big hands.
	You **have**	
	They **have**	

A What do you look like?

Read **and** Review

► **Write** the correct form of the verb *to have*.

► **Use** the *Look at Grammar* box to help you.

1. He _____ round eyes.

2. I _____ two long arms.

3. She _____ three short legs.

4. You _____ a small nose.

5. They _____ light hair.

6. We _____ one long tail.

7. You _____ big feet.

8. It _____ eight pointy claws.

Articles

- **A** before a consonant
  a small nose
- **An** before a vowel
  an orange nose
- **No article** before a plural noun
  noses

B Teammate descriptions

► **Observe** what you and your teammates look like.

► **Take** notes in the chart.

► **Write** your sentences.

► **Share** with your teammates.

Name	Adjective(s)	Body part	Sentence
(She) Ariane	two blue	eyes	She has two blue eyes.
(I)			
(You)			
(He)			
(She)			
(We)			
(They)			

C Differences and similarities

➤ **Find** the differences and the similarities between the two bodies.

➤ **Write** the differences and the similarities in the Venn diagram.

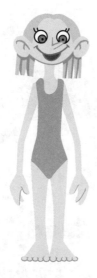 

She

small head

They

big ears

He

big head

D Talk about it

➤ **Take turns** sharing your findings from Activity C with your partner.

Read and Repeat

She has a small head. It's your turn.

They have big ears.

5 Clothing

A Clothing items

► **Repeat** the clothing items after your teacher.

L👀k at Words: Clothing

hat

running shoes

skirt

hoodie

shirt

socks

leggings

shoes

sweater

pants

shorts

T-shirt

B What are you wearing?

► **Describe** what you are wearing.

► **Use** the *Look at Words* box and the *Read and Repeat* box to help you.

Read and Repeat

> I am wearing a sweater, pants, socks and shoes.

_____

_____

_____

_____

_____

C Memory game

- ► **Look** at your partner's clothing then turn away from him or her.
- ► **Try** to remember what he or she is wearing.
- ► **Change** partners and **play** again.

Read and Repeat

What am I wearing?

No. I am wearing shorts.

You are wearing a T-shirt, pants and running shoes.

6 Describing clothing

A Listen

- ► **Listen** to the descriptions and **find** the correct picture.
- ► **Write** the letter in the box.

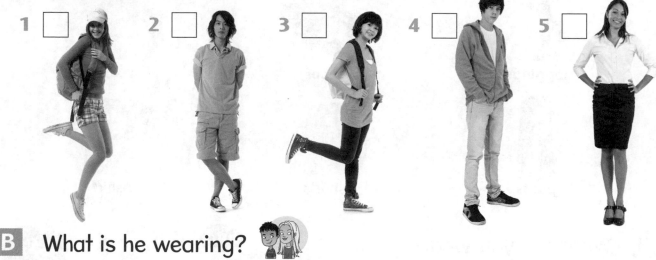

1 ☐   2 ☐   3 ☐   4 ☐   5 ☐

B What is he wearing?

- ► **Look** at the pictures in Activity A.
- ► **Write** what each person is wearing.

1. What is she wearing on her head?   She is wearing a white hat. _____

2. What is he wearing on his legs?   _____

3. What is she wearing on her feet?   _____

4. What is he wearing on his body?   _____

5. What is she wearing on her body?   _____

7 Story time

A Prepare to read

▶ **Skim** the story and **answer** the questions.

1. What is the title of the story?

_____

2. What is the story about? Circle your answer.

a) a birthday party

b) a costume party

c) a family get-together

3. What are the guests wearing? _____

L**👀**k at Words

bring: come to a place with something

guest: a person who is invited to your home

laugh: an action you do when something is funny

scared: full of fear, frightened

brave: ready for danger

B Story: Please Bring Your Monster!

▶ **Listen** to the story and **read** along.

❶ It is 3:30 and school is finished! Leo and his friends meet in the schoolyard. Leo gives them a party invitation. It says, "Please **bring** your monster." Eddie says, "I don't understand." Robin adds, "Monsters don't exist!" Leo explains his idea.

> I am having a costume party. Let's all wear monster costumes!

> That's a great idea, Leo!

2 The party is finally here! Ariane, Robin, Eddie and Lexie arrive at Leo's house. The **guests** look and **laugh** at their costumes. One monster says to the other, "Great costume! You have a big stomach!" The other monster answers, "Yes, and you have a long tail!"

I am wearing green leggings and a green sweater. What are you wearing?

I am wearing a red hat, a white T-shirt, blue pants and brown shoes.

3 The friends have fun at the party. They talk, dance, eat and play. Then, one monster points to the computer screen. "This website talks about real monsters! There is one called a sasquatch. It lives here, in Canada!" Another monster says, "Yes! It has a lot of hair, pointy teeth and long claws!" The friends look at the computer screen in silence. They are **scared**. Suddenly, they hear a sound.

What's that sound?

Listen! I hear something under the sofa!

4 "Can someone look?" asks a monster. Another monster answers, "Not me! I am scared!" They hear the sound again. Finally, one monster says, "Okay, I will look." The **brave** monster looks under the sofa and says, "I have it! I have the monster!" He takes something in his hands and shows it to the other monsters.

Ha, ha! My cat also likes costume parties!

C Show you understand

▶ **Scan** the story to find the answers.

1. Who organizes the party? _____

2. Name the five humans wearing monster costumes. _____

3. What is Leo wearing? _____

4. What are the two things that scare the friends? _____

_____

5. a) What is the name of the real monster in the story? _____

b) Describe it: _____

c) Do you think it exists? _____

6. Do you like costume parties? Why or why not? _____

_____

STOP and Think

I scan the story to find the answers. ○   I pay attention. ○   I don't understand everything and that's okay. ○

8 Learn and play

A Who is wearing what?

- ► **Take turns** reading the clues on the cards your teacher gives you.
- ► **Decide** which student is wearing which costume.
- ► **Write** the names of the students on the lines.

Costume 1

1. _____

Costume 2

2. _____

Costume 3

3. _____

Costume 4

4. _____

B Tic-tac-toe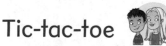

- ► **Describe** what you see using full sentences.
- ► **Place** an **X** or an **O** if your answer is correct.

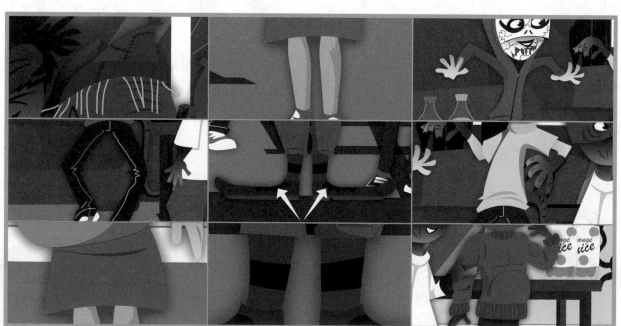

C The cat crossword

► **Write** the body parts in the crossword puzzle.

9 Link It Together

A Body parts: A race

► **Roll** the dice.

► **Draw** the body parts that correspond to the numbers.

► **Be** the first player to draw the 12 body parts first and **win** the game!

Head	Body
1. hair	**7.** arms
2. eyes	**8.** stomach
3. ears	**9.** hands
4. mouth	**10.** legs
5. nose	**11.** feet
6. tongue	**12.** tail

B I have three arms

► **Write** sentences using the verb *to have*.

► **Include** numbers and body parts.

1. (I)   I have three arms. _____

2. (he) _____

3. (they) _____

4. (we) _____

5. (she) _____

6. (you) _____

7. (it) _____

8. (I) _____

C Describing clothing

- ► **Highlight** the adjectives in the word bank.
- ► **Choose** an adjective and a clothing item.
- ► **Write** the combinations on the lines.
- ► **Use** articles (*a, an*) when needed.

sweater	red	pants	long
round	T-shirt	small	shoes
green	hat	dark	pointy
skirt	short	leggings	socks

1. a long skirt

2. _____

3. _____

4. _____

5. _____

6. _____

7. _____

8. _____

D Mix-pair-share

- ► **Tell** your partner what he or she is wearing.
- ► **Change** partners and repeat.

E The cat's costume description

- ► **Describe** the body and clothing of Leo's cat on page 43.
- ► **Use** adjectives, the verb *to have* and the expression "is wearing."

_____

_____

_____

_____

10 Project: My monster costume

A The plan

► **Choose** body parts, adjectives, clothing and colours for your monster costume.

► **Draw** your monster costume.

1. Choose <u>six</u> different body parts.

_____

_____

2. Choose a minimum of <u>four</u> different adjectives.

_____

_____

3. Choose <u>five</u> different clothing items.

_____

_____

4. Choose <u>five</u> different colours.

_____

_____

B The model

► **Look** at the model.

Monster Party Invitation

Come to my house for a costume party! Get ready to scare the guests with your monster costume!

This is my costume. I have a big head, a round nose and pointy ears. I have two short legs, small hands and big feet. I am wearing a red hat, a white T-shirt, blue pants, green socks and brown shoes.

Your friend, Leo

C ▶ The rough draft

► **Complete** your monster party invitation.

► **Use** your plan from Activity A and the model from Activity B to describe your monster costume.

Monster Party Invitation

Come to my house for a costume party! Get ready to scare the guests with your monster costume!

This is my costume. _____

_____

_____

_____

Your friend, _____

D ▶ The presentation

► **Look** at your partner's costume from Activity A.

► **Describe** your partner's costume to your teammates.

Read and Repeat

He has a big head, a round nose and two pointy ears. He is wearing a big red hat, a white T-shirt, blue pants, green socks and black shoes.

Very good! It's my turn.

Sign Me Up!

Recreation activities

basketball

judo

theatre

guitar

piano

painting

violin

hockey

dancing

swimming

Sign up at the community centre.

1 Recreation activities

A Let's have fun!

► **Look** at the Illustration.
► **Repeat** the recreation activities after your teacher.

B Interests

L(oo)k at Words: Interests

| arts | music | sports |

► **Match** the interests with the recreation activities in the chart below.
► **Use** the *Look at Words* box to help you.

Interest	Recreation activities	
	In the illustration	Other recreation activities you know
arts	dancing	
music		
sports		

> Let's create an advertisement for a recreation activity. Get your classmates to sign up for your activity.

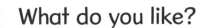

C What do you like?

► **Highlight** three recreation activities you like in the chart above.

2 Preferences

L👀k at Grammar: Asking questions in the present

We use the auxiliary verb *do* to ask questions in the present.

Preferences

Do you like painting?	Yes, I do. 😊
Do you like basketball?	No, I do not. / No, I don't. ☹

Other possibilities with *do*

Do you have hockey skates?	Yes, I do.

A Find a student who likes…

► **Ask** your classmates about recreation activities they like.

► **Write** their name on the line if they say "yes."

► **Use** the *Look at Grammar* box to help you.

1. painting _____

2. piano _____

3. hockey _____

4. dancing _____

5. swimming _____

6. violin _____

7. basketball _____

8. guitar _____

9. theatre _____

10. judo _____

B Compare preferences

► **Compare** the recreation activities you like with the recreation activities your classmates like.

► **Write** three preferences you share with your classmates.

► **Share** your sentences with your teammates.

Example: Ariane and I like theatre. Robin and I like judo. Eddie and I like piano.

1. _____

2. _____

3. _____

C Guess what I like

► **Choose** five recreation activities and **write** them in the chart.

► **Ask** your partner which interest he or she likes.

► **Ask** your partner which recreation activity he or she likes.

► **Be** the first player to guess the recreation activity and **win** the game!

Read and Repeat

Do you like arts?

Yes, I do. Do you like sports?

Yes, I do. Do you like theatre?

Yes, I do. You win!

Game	My recreation activity	My partner's recreation activity	Winner
	theatre	hockey	Robin
1			
2			
3			
4			
5			

D Leo's interview

► **Listen** to Leo interview his friends.

► **Write** the recreation activities in the correct column.

Name	I like 😃	I don't like 😞
1. Leo		
2. Ariane		
3. Eddie		
4. Lexie		
5. Robin		

3 Types of recreation activities

A I like physical activities!

► **Repeat** the types of recreation activities after your teacher.

L👀k at Words: Types of recreation activities

| physical | non-physical | group |
| individual | indoor | outdoor |

B Check it out!

► **Put** a check (✓) for each type of recreation activity.

	Physical	Non-physical	Group	Individual	Indoor	Outdoor
basketball	✓		✓		✓	✓
dancing						
guitar						
hockey						
judo						
painting						
piano						
swimming						
theatre						
violin						

C Do you like…?

Step 1

- ► **Ask** your partner which types of activities he or she likes.
- ► **Put** a check mark next to your partner's preferences.
- ► **Use** the *Read and Repeat* box to help you.

Types of activities	✓
physical	
non-physical	
group	
individual	
indoor	
outdoor	

Read and Repeat

Do you like physical activities?

Yes, I do.

Read and Review

Third person singular

He **likes** group activities.

She **likes** indoor activities.

Step 2

- ► **Look** at your partner's answers.
- ► **Write** a description of the types of activities he or she likes.

Leo	Leo likes physical, group, indoor and outdoor activities.
Partner's name	
Partner's name	

D Your suggestions

- ► **Look** at your partner's answers in Activity C.
- ► **Think** of a recreation activity your partner can sign up for.
- ► **Use** Activity B to help you.
- ► **Suggest** your idea to your partner.

Read and Repeat

Great idea!

You like physical, group, indoor and outdoor activities. Sign up for swimming!

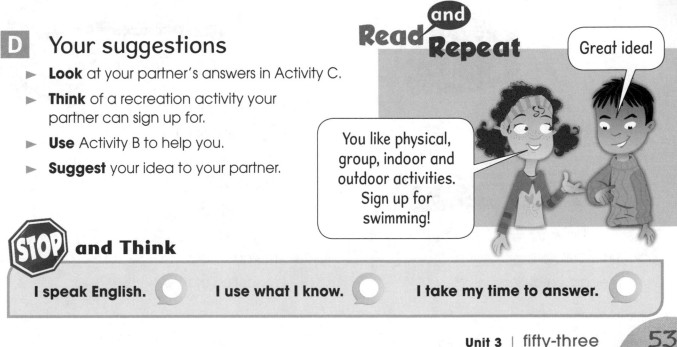

STOP and Think

I speak English. ○	I use what I know. ○	I take my time to answer. ○

4 When does it start?

L👀k at Grammar: Prepositions of time

We use *at*, *on* and *in* to indicate time.

Prepositions	Time categories	Examples
at	time	I have judo **at** 6:00.
on	day	I have judo **on** Wednesday.
	date	I have judo **on** January 8.
in	part of day	I have judo **in** the afternoon.
	month	I have judo **in** January.
	season	I have judo **in** winter.

A It's time for fun!

► **Look** at the pictures below.

► **Write** the time category and the preposition of time under each picture.

► **Use** the *Look at Grammar* box to help you.

1. Time category: date

   Preposition of time: on

2. Time category: _____

   Preposition of time: _____

3. Time category: _____

   Preposition of time: _____

4. Time category: _____

   Preposition of time: _____

5. Time category: _____

   Preposition of time: _____

6. Time category: _____

   Preposition of time: _____

B Ariane's schedule

- ► **Take turns** reading the sentences below.
- ► **Write** the correct prepositions of time.
- ► **Use** the *Look at Grammar* box on page 54 to help you.

Hi, I am Ariane! I like music and arts. I sign up for piano ₁__in__ **autumn** and for theatre

₂_____ **winter**. Piano starts ₃_____ **September 12** and finishes ₄_____ **December 11**.

It is ₅_____ **Wednesday** ₆_____ **7:00**. Theatre starts ₇_____ **January**. It is ₈_____ the

morning, ₉_____ **Saturday**. It is ₁₀_____ **9:00**. ₁₁_____ **summer**, I sign up for painting.

It starts ₁₂_____ **June 26**. It is ₁₃_____ **the afternoon**, ₁₄_____ **1:00**, ₁₅_____ **Tuesday**.

I am very excited!

C What is your schedule?

- ► **Complete** the information in the agenda, using the cards your teacher gives you.
- ► **Ask** your partner about his or her schedule.

Read and Repeat

Do you have hockey in winter?

Do you have hockey in January?

Yes, I do.

Yes, I do!

Student A: Swimming lessons	Student B: Theatre lessons
Season: _____	Season: _____
Months: _____	Months: _____
_____	_____
Day: _____	Day: _____
Part of the day: _____	Part of the day: _____
_____	_____
Time: _____	Time: _____

5 Places for recreation activities

A Get ready and go!

► **Repeat** the places for recreation activities after your teacher.

L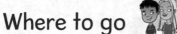k at Words: Places for recreation activities

arena

community centre

pool

school

studio

B Where to go

► **Write** the places you go for each recreation activity.

► **Use** the *Look at Words* box to help you.

Name	Recreation activity	Places
Ariane	piano	
Robin	guitar	
Lexie	dancing	
Eddie	swimming	

C I go to the...

► **Listen** to the students talk about where they go for their recreation activities.

► **Circle** the correct place in Activity B.

6 Going places

L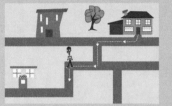k at Grammar: Prepositions of place

We use *to* and *at* when we talk about a place.

to: shows movement in the direction of a place

Eddie goes **to** the judo studio on Fridays.

at: identifies a place or where something happens

Eddie is **at** the judo studio.

A *At* or *to*?

► **Write** the correct preposition of place.

► **Use** the *Look at Grammar* box to help you.

1. I go ___to___ Da Vinci Studio for painting class.

2. Lexie walks _____ the studio for dancing.

3. Robin's basketball practice is _____ Greenwood School.

4. Tonight, I have violin _____ the community centre.

5. Eddie's mom drives _____ the judo studio.

6. On Tuesday, Ariane has piano _____ Greenwood School.

7. Lexie goes _____ the arena for hockey practice.

8. Ariane has theatre _____ Parker Studio.

B Prepositions board game

► **Roll** the die to move around the game board.

► **Read** the expression of time or place in the square you land on.

► **Complete** the sentence with the correct preposition of time or place.

► **Be** the first player to get to *Finish* and **win** the game!

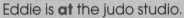

Read **and** Repeat

It says "April 8."
Painting is **on** April 8.

That's right!
It's my turn.

7 Story time

A Prepare to read

► **Skim** the story and **answer** the questions.

1. What is the title of the story? _____

2. What is this story about? Circle the correct answer.

   a) Leo and his mother want to go on vacation.

   b) Leo wants to sign up for recreation activities.

   c) Leo wants to do an activity with his mother.

3. What recreation activities do you do?

_____

B Story: Help Me Choose!

► **Listen** to the story and **read** along.

① Leo comes home from school and sits down to watch TV. He is **bored**. His mother comes in holding a guide with recreation activities in her hands. "Leo, look! We have a guide with recreation activities you can sign up for."

"That's great, Mom! Let's look at it together."

② Leo's mother helps him find a recreation activity. "Do you like sports?" Leo answers, "Yes, I do. I like group activities." His mother asks, "Do you like arts?" Leo answers, "Yes, I do, but I don't like dancing." "Do you like music, Leo?" "Yes, I do, but I don't like violin," answers Leo. His mother asks, "Do you like indoor or outdoor activities?" Leo answers, "I like both!"

3 Leo tells his mother, "I want to sign up for hockey, basketball, guitar, painting and theatre." His mother answers, "No, Leo. You can sign up for one recreation activity in winter and a different one in spring."

4 Leo's mother tells him that he has to **respect** their family schedule too. His activity has to be on Monday, Wednesday or Friday. He has to sign up for an activity that is in the evening. Also, the activity needs to be at the school, the community centre or the arena.

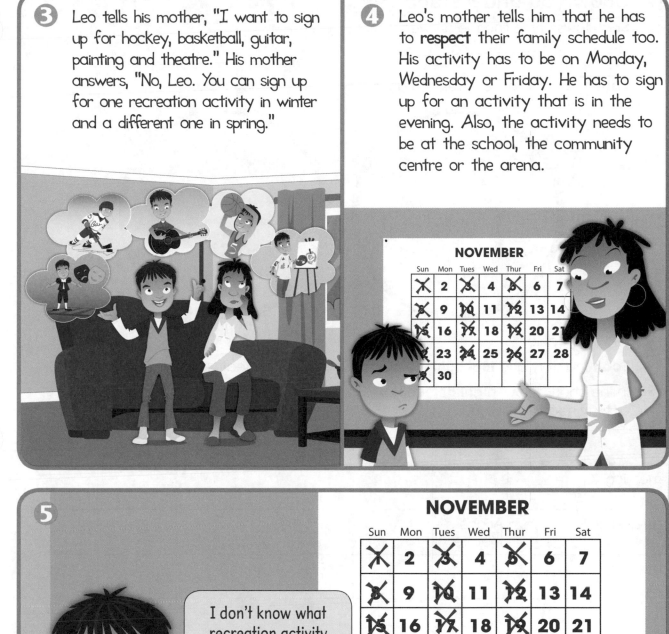

5

I don't know what recreation activity to sign up for! Can you help me? And I want to sign up with one of my friends too!

NOVEMBER

Sun	Mon	Tues	Wed	Thur	Fri	Sat
1	2	3	4	5	6	7
8	9	10	11	12	13	14
15	16	17	18	19	20	21
22	23	24	25	26	27	28
29	30					

STOP and Think

I scan the story to find the answers. I pay attention. I don't understand everything and that's okay.

C Show you understand

► **Scan** the story to find the answers.

1. Leo's preferences

► **Write** the activities Leo likes and doesn't like in the correct circle.

2. Leo's schedule

► **Scan** the story and **highlight** the places where Leo's recreation activity needs to be.

► In the chart below, **highlight** the boxes of the days and parts of the day that Leo's activity needs to be on.

	Sunday	Monday	Tuesday	Wednesday	Thursday	Friday	Saturday
morning							
afternoon		Ariane: theatre					
evening							

3. Leo's activity

► **Read** the clues below.

► **Write** the friends' names and activities in the chart above.

► **Write** the activity and the name of the friend Leo can sign up with in the sentence below.

Ariane goes to the community centre for theatre in the afternoon on Monday.

Eddie goes to the pool for swimming in the afternoon on Saturday.

Robin has basketball at Greenwood School in the evening on Wednesday and Friday.

Lexie has hockey at the arena in the morning on Tuesday and Thursday.

Leo's activity is _____. He can sign up with _____.

8 Learn and play

A Scrambled places

► **Unscramble** the places for recreation activities.

► **Write** the answer on the line.

1. lcaep

place

2. oshocl

3. itodsu

4. nreaa

5. sstpor rneetc

6. mtoumciyn etnecr

7. olpo

B I like swimming!

► **Read** the clues below.

► **Write** the words in the puzzle.

Across

1. a type of activity

4. a type of activity

5. an interest

Down

1. a place

2. a type of activity

3. a preposition of place

C Which does not belong?

► **Read** the combinations.

► **Circle** the word that does not belong.

Example: painting /(basketball)/ theatre

1. swimming / hockey / theatre

2. dancing / judo / painting

3. Monday / evening / Sunday

4. April / morning / afternoon

5. violin / judo / basketball

6. guitar / piano / hockey

7. spring / winter / May

8. September 3 / 8:00 / December 4

9  Link It Together

A Your recreation activity

▶ **Choose** a recreation activity you like and decide when you like to do it.

▶ **Write** it in the chart below.

▶ **Describe** your activity and schedule, using the interest, recreation activity and time expression that go along with it.

Month: _____

	Sunday	Monday	Tuesday	Wednesday	Thursday	Friday	Saturday
morning							
afternoon	dancing 1:00						
evening					dancing 7:00		

I like arts. I like dancing. It is an indoor, physical and group activity. It is in winter, in February. It is on Sunday, in the afternoon, at 1:00 and on Thursday, in the evening, at 7:00.

_____

_____

_____

B Let's sign up! Read and Repeat

▶ **Ask** your partner what recreation activity he or she likes.

▶ **Look** at your schedule in Activity A.

▶ **Circle** the boxes showing when you can sign up for your activity together.

Do you like dancing?

Yes, I do!

We can sign up on Wednesday, in the afternoon.

That's a great idea!

STOP and Think

I use resources. ◯   **I cooperate.** ◯   **I take risks.** ◯

C Leo's basketball schedule

► **Describe** Leo's schedule.

► **Use** prepositions of time and time categories.

January

Sunday	Monday	Tuesday	Wednesday	Thursday	Friday	Saturday
				1	2	3
4	5	6	7	8	9	10
11	12	13	14	15	16	17
18	19	20	21	22	23	24
25	26	27	28	29	30	31

	Prepositions of time	Time categories
1. season	in	winter
2. month		
3. days		
4. dates	not	
5. time		

D Places

► **Write** the correct preposition of place on the first line.

► **Write** a possible place for the recreation activity on the second line.

1. They have painting __at__ the ____community centre____ .

2. She goes _____ the _____ for swimming.

3. Basketball is _____ Greenwood _____ .

4. For tournaments, Leo and Robin go _____ a different _____ .

5. He goes _____ the _____ for judo.

6. Lexie plays hockey _____ the _____ .

7. My theatre class is _____ Parker _____ .

8. We go _____ the_____ for violin.

9. Ariane takes piano _____ Greenwood _____ .

10 Project: Please sign up!

A The plan

► **Choose** a recreation activity.

► **Complete** the mind map.

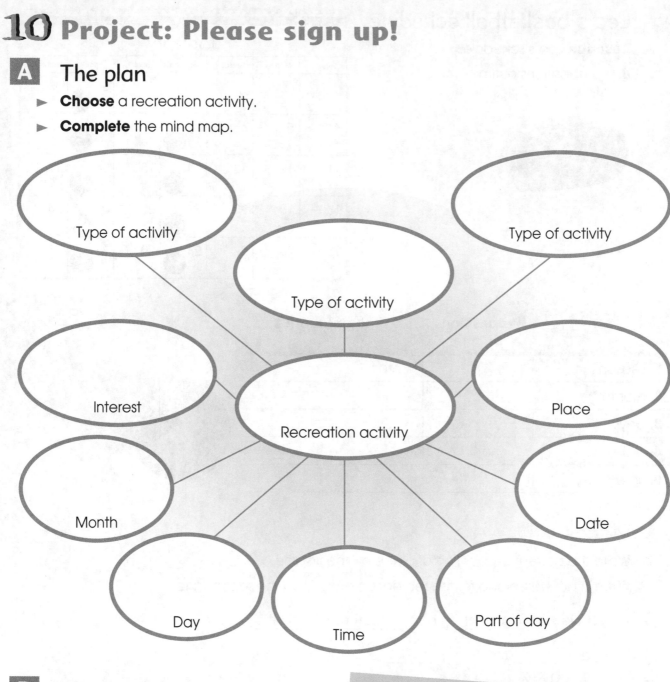

Type of activity

Type of activity

Type of activity

Interest

Place

Recreation activity

Month

Date

Day

Time

Part of day

B The model

► **Look** at the model advertisement.

► **Highlight** the prepositions of time and place.

► **Use** one colour for prepositions of time and a different colour for the preposition of place.

Sign up for judo!

Do you like sports?

Do you like physical activities?

Do you like group activities?

Do you like indoor activities?

Sign up for judo in January at Parker Studio!

Judo is on Tuesday, in the evening, at 7:00.

Judo starts on January 8!

C The rough draft

► **Write** your advertisement.

► **Use** your plan from Activity A and the model from Activity B to help you.

_____

_____

_____

_____

D The presentation

Step 1

► **Read** the advertisements posted in your classroom.

► **Sign up** for two recreation activities.

► **Write** notes in the chart about the activities.

Activity	Place	Time
swimming	pool	March Monday 7:00 evening
Activity 1	**Place**	**Time**
Activity 2	**Place**	**Time**

Step 2

► **Share** the information with your teammates.

Read and Repeat

I go to the pool to swim. The lessons are in March, on Monday, at 7:00 in the evening.

1 At the potluck

A Celebrate!

► **Look** at the illustration.

► **Circle** the correct answer.

1. The students are at a restaurant for a night out.

2. The students are at a potluck for a special celebration.

3. The students are at a cooking class with their parents.

B Potluck menu

► **Look** at the illustration.

► **Repeat** the **types of dishes** and the **meals** after your teacher.

► **Write** the **types of dishes** and the **meals** on the potluck menu card.

| Potluck menu card ||
Types of dishes	Meals
soups	vegetable soup pea soup

Note: Juice, water and soft drinks are not dishes or meals. They are _____ .

fruit salad

cake

water

juice

soft drinks

cookies

drinks

Let's have a potluck and celebrate! Prepare a potluck and describe your menu.

C Reasons to celebrate

► **Write** two reasons to have a potluck.

Example: We have a potluck to celebrate a birthday.

1. _____

2. _____

2 Food guide

A Food groups

► **Repeat** the four food groups after your teacher.

l👀k at Words: Food groups

Vegetables and fruit

broccoli	carrots	lettuce	mushrooms	onions
peas	peppers	potatoes	spinach	tomatoes
apples	bananas	blackberries	grapes	kiwis
oranges	peaches	pineapples	raspberries	strawberries

Grain products

bagels	bread	cereal	couscous	muffins
oats	pasta	pita bread	rice	tortillas

Milk and alternatives

cheese   kefir   milk   soy beverage   yogourt

Meat and alternatives

beans   beef   chicken   eggs   fish

ham   nuts   pork   tofu

B Mealtime

▶ **Read** the ingredients for each meal.

▶ **Write** which food group is missing.

▶ **Add** another ingredient to make up the four food groups.

▶ **Use** the *Look at Words* box on pages 68 and 69 to help you.

Read and **Repeat**

> I think the missing food group is grain products.

> I agree! Let's add cereal to the meal.

1. Meal: macaroni and cheese

Ingredients: pasta, tomatoes, cheese

Missing food group: _____

Another ingredient: _____

2. Meal: falafel sandwiches

Ingredients: pita bread, beans, lettuce

Missing food group: _____

Another ingredient: _____

3. Meal: pea soup

Ingredients: ham, peas, onions, milk

Missing food group: _____

Another ingredient: _____

4. Meal: pasta salad

Ingredients: pasta, beans, peppers

Missing food group: _____

Another ingredient: _____

3 Describing things

Lk at Grammar: Describing things

We use **there is** and **there are** to describe things.

Singular

There is beef in the enchiladas.

There is vegetable soup on the table.

Plural

There are eggs in the cake.

There are cookies on the table.

A Time to eat!

► **Write** *There is* or *There are* beside the ingredients below.

► **Use** the *Look at Grammar* box to help you.

1. What is in sushi?

a) There is _____ rice.

b) _____ fish.

c) _____ vegetables.

2. What is in pasta salad?

a) _____ peppers.

b) _____ pasta.

c) _____ tomatoes.

3. What is in green salad?

a) _____ spinach.

b) _____ carrots.

c) _____ tofu.

4. What is in couscous salad?

a) _____ couscous.

b) _____ peppers.

c) _____ tofu.

5. What is in enchiladas?

a) _____ cheese.

b) _____ tomatoes.

c) _____ beef.

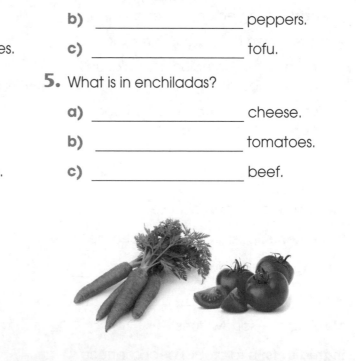

STOP and Think

I take risks. ◯   I use what I know. ◯   I ask for help or clarification. ◯

B Your four meals

► **Draw** four different meals on a separate piece of paper.

► **Describe** your meals to your teammates.

► **Use** the *Look at Grammar* box on page 70 to help you.

4 Possessives

Lk at Grammar: Possessives

We use **'s** to indicate possession. We place it after nouns and names.

my friend**'s** yogourt   Ben**'s** cereal

A Who does this belong to?

► **Write** the food and who it belongs to.

► **Use** the *Look at Grammar* box to help you.

1. It is Eddie's apple.

2. _____

3. _____

4. _____

5. _____

6. _____

B Food favourites

- **Review** the foods in the four food groups on pages 68 and 69.
- **Write** one favourite food from each food group on the lines below.
- **Ask** your classmates about their favourite food from the four food groups.
- **Write** their answers in the chart.

Your favourites

Milk and alternatives _____

Vegetables and fruit _____

Meat and alternatives _____

Grain products _____

Read and **Review**

Preferences

Ariane's favourite food is raspberries.

Read and **Repeat**

What is your favourite food from the vegetables and fruit group?

My favourite food from the vegetables and fruit group is raspberries.

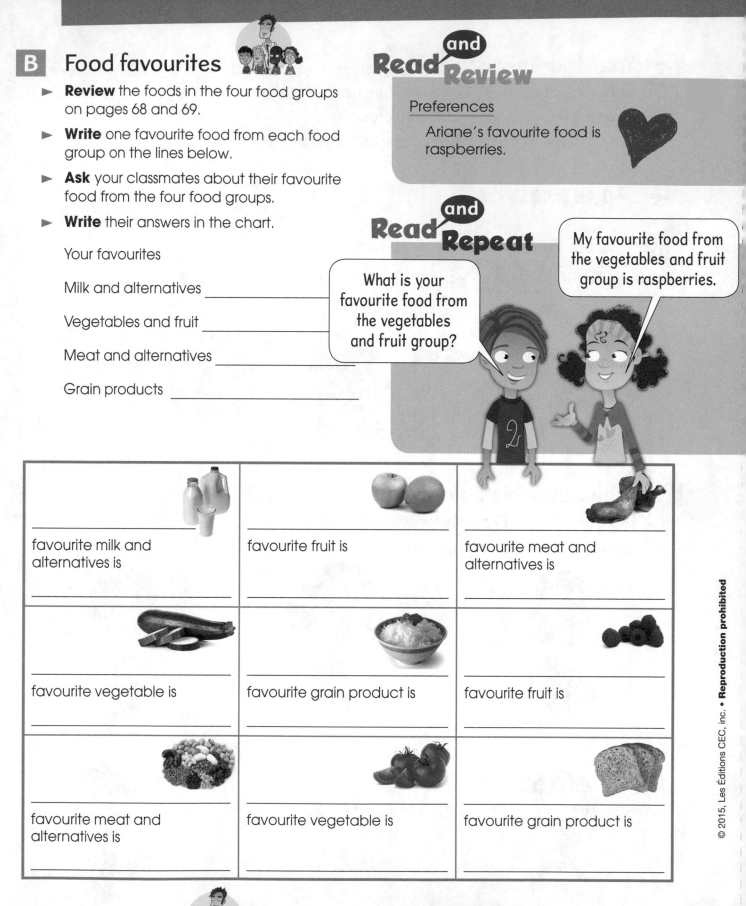

favourite milk and alternatives is _____	favourite fruit is _____	favourite meat and alternatives is _____
favourite vegetable is _____	favourite grain product is _____	favourite fruit is _____
favourite meat and alternatives is _____	favourite vegetable is _____	favourite grain product is _____

C Food bingo

- **Listen** to your teacher and **play** the game.

5 My food

L👀k at Grammar: Possessive adjectives

We use possessive adjectives to indicate possession.

Subject pronouns

Singular: I | you | he | she | it

Plural: we | you | they

Possessive adjectives

Singular: my | your | his | her | its

Plural: our | your | their

A Fruit salad!

► **Highlight** the possessive adjectives.

► **Draw** an arrow from the subject pronouns to the possessive adjectives.

I have an orange. It is my orange. You have a pineapple. It is your pineapple.

He has strawberries. They are his strawberries. She has grapes. They are her grapes.

You and Lexie have bananas. They are your bananas. Ariane and Leo have apples.

They are their apples. We made a dessert with all of our fruit. Look at our fruit salad!

B Possessive adjectives practice

► **Replace** the highlighted words with the correct possessive adjective.
► **Use** the *Look at Grammar* box on page 73 to help you.

1. Ariane eats a kiwi.

It is ___her___ kiwi.

2. Eddie eats broccoli.

It is _____ broccoli.

3. Lexie and I make pea soup.

It is _____ pea soup.

4. I have a glass of juice.

It is _____ glass of juice.

5. She eats a cheese sandwich.

It is _____ cheese sandwich.

6. The dog eats dog food.

It is _____ food.

7. Leo has a muffin.

It is _____ muffin.

8. Eddie eats cookies with Leo.

They are _____ cookies.

9. You have macaroni and cheese for lunch.

It is _____ macaroni and cheese.

10. You and your family make bread.

It is _____ bread.

C Who likes what?

► **Listen** to the students' preferences.
► **Write** the students' preferences using possessive adjectives.
► **Write** the correct letter.

A	sushi	D	cake
B	couscous salad	E	pea soup
C	soy beverage	F	cheese sandwiches

1. [A] ___Its___ favourite main dish is _____sushi_____.

2. [ ] _____ favourite soup is _____.

3. [ ] _____ favourite dessert is _____.

4. [ ] _____ favourite salad is _____.

5. [ ] _____ favourite drink is _____.

6. [ ] _____ favourite sandwiches are _____.

6 Describing food

A Delicious

► **Repeat** the food adjectives after your teacher.

L👀k at Words: Food adjectives

healthy: good for your body

delicious: good to taste

crunchy

soft

salty

sweet

hot

cold

B Food descriptions

► **Read** the sentences below.

► **Write** the correct food adjective.

1. There is sugar in Lexie's cookies. Her cookies are _____ sweet _____.

2. Carrots are _____. They make noise when we eat them.

3. Be careful! Robin's enchiladas are very _____!

4. There is too much salt in Eddie's soup. His soup is _____.

5. There is tofu and spinach in Ariane's salad. Her salad is _____.

6. Leo's cake is so _____. It melts in your mouth!

7. Lexie's fruit salad is _____. It is in the refrigerator.

8. Ariane and Lexie's muffins are very good. Their muffins are _____!

9. Desserts are _____. I love to eat them sometimes.

C Think-pair-share

► **Describe** eight different foods with your partner.

► **Use** the adjectives in the *Look at Words* box on page 75.

► **Write** your descriptions below.

► **Share** your food descriptions with the rest of your team.

Read and Repeat

Bananas are delicious.

I agree! They are also sweet.

1. Bananas are delicious and sweet. _____
2. _____
3. _____
4. _____
5. _____
6. _____
7. _____
8. _____

D Lexie's meals

► **Take turns** reading the clues on the cards your teacher gives you.

► **Decide** what meals Lexie has on her plate.

► **Write** the meals on the lines.

Read and Repeat

I think the answer is couscous salad.

I disagree. I think it is green salad.

1. _____
2. _____
3. _____
4. _____
5. _____
6. _____

7 Story time

A Prepare to read

▶ **Skim** the story and **answer** the questions.

1. What is the title of the story? _____

2. What is this story about? Circle your answer.

  a) Lexie's friends don't want to play with her.

  b) Lexie's friends teach their parents to cook.

  c) Lexie's friends organize a potluck.

  d) It's Lexie's birthday.

3. Name two meals you see in the story.

L👀k at Words

best: the most excellent

disappointed: sad that something didn't happen

busy: occupied with an activity

B Story: Lexie's Surprise

▶ **Listen** to the story and **read** along.

It's Saturday afternoon. Lexie is in her bedroom. She looks at her new hockey medal. On her medal, it says **"Best Team Player."**

Lexie goes into the kitchen to show her medal to her parents. They tell her they are too busy to look at it. They are making falafel sandwiches.

Her mother suggests, "Call your friend, Leo. You can play together."

Lexie answers, "Okay, I'll call him," but she is **disappointed**.

Lexie calls Leo. She invites him to play.

Leo says, "Sorry. I am **busy** now. Lexie, what's your favourite salad?"

Lexie answers, "Pasta salad with red peppers and cheese! It's crunchy and soft! Why do you ask?"

Leo answers, "No reason. Bye, Lexie."

Eddie and his mother make a healthy vegetable soup.

Eddie's mother says, "Let's see... There are onions and carrots and there is pasta and spinach."

They hear the sound of the video call.

Eddie says, "Oh no, it's Lexie! Don't answer that."

Ariane and her mother make a fruit salad.

Ariane's mother says, "Our dessert is sweet!" Ariane says, "Let's add strawberries! They are her favourite fruit."

The telephone rings. Ariane says, "Oh no, it's Lexie. I can't answer the phone!"

Robin and his parents make enchiladas.

Robin says, "Lexie and I love enchiladas. It is our favourite meal! Enchiladas are delicious!"

They hear a knock at the door. Robin says, "Oh no, it's Lexie. Don't answer the door. She will ask why we are making so many enchiladas!"

Lexie walks home. She is sad.

She opens the door and hears "Surprise!" Lexie's family and friends are there.

Lexie's mother says, "We want to celebrate your hockey medal."

Lexie's father adds, "Everybody made a meal so we can celebrate together!"

Lexie says, "Thank you! What a great surprise!"

C Show you understand

▶ **Scan** the story to find the answers.

1. Why do the friends organize a potluck?

_____

2. Complete Lexie's dad's notes.

Potluck menu: Lexie's favourite meals

Meal	Friend's name
1. _____	_____
2. _____	_____
3. _____	_____
4. _____	_____

3. What is Robin and Lexie's favourite meal? _____

4. Complete Lexie's thank-you notes with the name of the person and the correct adjectives.

a) Thank you, _____, for your _____ enchiladas.

b) Thank you, _____, for your _____ fruit salad.

c) Thank you, _____, for your _____ soup.

d) Thank you, ____, for your _____ and pasta salad.

5. Write the name of a meal from the story for each food group.

Vegetables and fruit: _____   Milk and alternatives: _____

Grain products: _____   Meat and alternatives: _____

6. What meal do you make at home?

_____

STOP and Think

| I use what I know. ○ | I pay attention. ○ | I don't understand everything and that's okay. ○ |

8 Link It Together

A Food art

▶ **Describe** the food you see.

▶ **Use** *There is* and *There are*.

1. There are bananas. _____

2. _____

3. _____

4. _____

5. _____

B Melting pot

▶ **Choose** one food from each of the four food groups.

▶ **Write** four different adjectives to describe the four foods.

1. Food group: _____

Food: _____

Adjective: _____

2. Food group: _____

Food: _____

Adjective: _____

3. Food group: _____

Food: _____

Adjective: _____

4. Food group: _____

Food: _____

Adjective: _____

C Possessive adjectives

▶ **Replace** the highlighted words with the correct possessive adjective.

1. I drink juice. It is _____ glass of juice.

2. We love enchiladas. _____ favourite meal is enchiladas.

3. You have a very salty soup. _____ soup needs more water.

4. Ariane's green salad has many vegetables. _____ salad is crunchy.

5. Robin's fruit salad is healthy. _____ fruit salad is good for you.

6. Leo's friends make delicious meals. _____ meals taste great.

7. You and your friends love beans. _____ favourite meat and alternatives are beans.

8. Leo's cat likes to drink. _____ favourite drink is water.

D At the potluck

▶ **Write** about the meals you see.

▶ **Use** *there is, there are* and *'s*.

▶ **Decide** which meal is your favourite and **complete** the sentences below.

▶ **Share** with your partner.

Example: In Lexie's meal, there is a cheese sandwich, green salad and there are cookies.

1. _____

2. _____

3. _____

4. _____

My favourite meal is _____ meal.
possessive name

_____ meal is _____,
possessive adjective   adjective

_____ and _____.
adjective   adjective

STOP **and Think**

I cooperate. ◯   **I infer.** ◯   **I use resources.** ◯

9 Project: Prepare your own potluck

A The plan

▶ **Choose** a meal to prepare for your potluck.

▶ **Write** about your meal.

Meal: _____

The foods that are in your meal: _____

_____

The food groups that are in your meal: _____

Three adjectives to describe your meal: _____

B The model

▶ **Look** at the model.

▶ **Circle** the adjectives.

▶ **Box** the food groups.

▶ **Highlight** *there is* in one colour and *there are* in a different colour.

I am bringing a soup to the potluck.

My meal is vegetable soup. It is healthy and hot.

My vegetable soup has vegetables. There is spinach. There are tomatoes and carrots.

My vegetable soup has meat and alternatives. In my soup, there are beans.

My vegetable soup has grain products. There is pasta in my soup.

It looks delicious!

C The rough draft

▶ **Use** your plan from Activity A and the model from Activity B to write about your meal.

▶ **Circle** the adjectives.

▶ **Box** the food groups.

▶ **Highlight** *there is* in one colour and *there are* in a different colour.

I am bringing _____ to the potluck. _____

_____

_____

_____

_____ It looks delicious!

D The presentation

Step 1

► **Draw** your meal on a separate sheet of paper.

► **Write** the name of your meal at the top of the sheet.

► **Describe** your meal with two or three adjectives.

► **Label** the foods that are in your meal.

Vegetable Soup

My soup is healthy and hot.

spinach

carrots

pasta

tomatoes

beans

Lexie

Step 2

► **Take turns** describing your partner's meal.

Step 3

► **Go** around the potluck table.

► **Describe** your classmates' meals to your partner.

Read and Repeat

Your meal is vegetable soup. Your soup is healthy and hot. In your soup, there is spinach and pasta. There are tomatoes, carrots and beans.

That's right. It's my turn.

Read and Repeat

Robin's meal is enchiladas. His enchiladas are hot and delicious. In his enchiladas, there is beef and lettuce. There are tomatoes.

Step 4

► **Choose** four meals to "place" in your plate.

Bon appétit!

1 Schoolyard activities

A Let's play!

► **Look** at the illustration.

► **Repeat** the schoolyard words after your teacher.

1. What else is in the picture?

_____

_____

2. What's the problem in the Greenwood schoolyard?

_____

B Greenwood schoolyard

► **Look** at the schoolyard with a partner.

► **Write** the activities that work.

► **Write** the activities that need to be repaired.

Activities that work	Activities that need to be repaired

C Your own schoolyard

► **Highlight** the activities in the chart in Activity B that you have in your own schoolyard.

► **Share** your answers with the class.

hopscotch

hula hoop

The schoolyard needs to be repaired! Help my friends and me create a perfect schoolyard.

2 Schoolyard actions

A Let's get moving!

► **Read** the action words and the activity words in the *Look at Words* box.

► **Write** the action and the activity under each picture.

L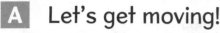at Words

Actions	catch	climb	jump	play	run	throw

Activities	balls	running track	basketball	target
	climbing wall	hopscotch		

1. Action: _____

Activity: _____

2. Action: _____

Activity: _____

3. Action: _____

Activity: _____

4. Action: _____

Activity: _____

5. Action: _____

Activity: _____

6. Action: _____

Activity: _____

3 I can do it!

L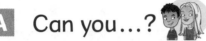k at Grammar: Capabilities

We use *can* to talk about capability.

Question	Affirmative	Negative
Can you catch?	Yes, I **can**.	No, I **cannot**. / No, I **can't**.
Can she jump?	Yes, she **can**.	No, she **cannot**. / No, she **can't**.
Can he throw?	Yes, he **can**.	No, he **cannot**. / No, he **can't**.

A | Can you…?

- ► **Ask** your partner if he or she can do schoolyard actions.
- ► **Use** the language in the *Read and Repeat* box to help you.
- ► **Mime** the action.

B | He can! He can't!

- ► **Take turns** reading your card to your teammates.
- ► **Write** the information in the chart.
- ► **Suggest** an activity for each character.

Read and Repeat

Can you run?　Yes, I can!　Can you climb?　No, I can't.

Student	Ariane	Eddie	Lexie	Robin
Capability				
Action				
Activity				

STOP and Think

I speak English. ○ I use what I know. ○ I take risks. ○

4 Story time

A Prepare to read

▶ **Skim** the story and **answer** the questions.

1. What is the title of the story? _____

2. What is this story about? Circle your answer.

   a) The students prepare a birthday party.

   b) The students of Greenwood School raise money to repair the activities in their schoolyard.

   c) The students don't want to play at recess.

3. What do the students sell? _____

L👀k at Words

recess time: break time for students

deflated: no air in a ball

bake sale: an event where baked food is sold

sell: exchange something for money

B Story: Let's Repair Our Schoolyard!

▶ **Listen** to the story and **read** along.

❶ It's **recess time** at Greenwood School. Lexie, Ariane, Eddie and Robin walk around the schoolyard to find an activity to do. Many of the activities need to be repaired. They go talk to Ms. Elisabeth.

> Ms. Elisabeth, I can throw very well but I can't throw balls at the target anymore! The circles are not visible.

> I like to play ball, but look! Many balls are **deflated**!

> I can't play basketball. There is no net.

> I want to run around the running track but I can't see the lines clearly!

> This is not fun. Wait! I have an idea!

2 The next day, Mr. O'Dell and Ms. Goldberg come into Ms. Elisabeth's classroom. Mr. O'Dell says, "Hello everyone! We have an important project to talk to you about. Do you all know Ms. Goldberg?"

"Yes!" answer the students. Robin adds,

3 "She is Eddie's grandmother and she planted the flowers in our schoolyard."

Ms. Goldberg answers, "That's right, Robin! Today, I am here to help you repair your schoolyard!" The students are excited and yell, "Hurray!"

Now, please tell me what needs to be repaired.

We will have to work together. It's going to take some teamwork!

4 To help raise money to repair the schoolyard, Ms. Goldberg, Mr. O'Dell, the teachers and the students all agree to have a **bake sale**. They will **sell** cupcakes! The students are very happy to participate in this project.

5 The day of the sale, the students bring their cupcakes to school. They put up posters on the school walls and they decorate the entrance.

"Great teamwork!" says Ariane.

To be continued...

Wow! Look at all the people! We can sell so many cupcakes!

CUPCAKES
$ 2.00

Show you understand

► **Scan** the story to find the answers.

1. The students cannot find an activity to do. Why? Circle the correct answer.
   a) The students don't like the activities in their schoolyard.
   b) The students have no imagination.
   c) Many activities need to be repaired.

2. What activities can't Ariane, Robin, Eddie and Lexie do? Complete the sentences.
   a) Ariane can't _____
   b) Robin can't _____
   c) Eddie can't _____
   d) Lexie can't _____

3. Why does the school have a bake sale?
   _____

4. Name the people who agree to have a bake sale.
   _____

5. Who helps repair the schoolyard? Circle the correct answer.
   a) The students
   b) Ms. Golderg
   c) Mr. O'Dell
   d) Ms. Elisabeth

6. On the day of the bake sale, what do the students do to help?
   _____
   _____
   _____

7. Are there activities in your schoolyard that need to be repaired?
   _____

   If yes, which ones?
   _____

STOP and Think

| I scan the story to find the answers. | I pay attention. | I don't understand everything and that's okay. |

5 Where is it?

Lk at Grammar: Prepositions of position

We use prepositions of position to show where one thing is in relation to another.

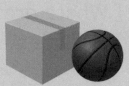

The basketball is **in** the box.

The basketball is **on** the box.

The basketball is **under** the box.

The basketball is **next to** the box.

The basketball is **in front of** the box.

The basketball is **behind** the box.

The basketball is **between** the two boxes.

A Where things are

► **Look** at the schoolyard on pages 84 and 85.

► **Complete** the sentences with the correct prepositions of position.

1. The balls are _____in_____ the basket.

2. The slide is _____ the monkey bars and the tunnel.

3. A tree is _____ the tunnel.

4. Eddie is _____ the basketball net.

5. The spider web is _____ the jungle gym.

6. The garbage can is _____ the hopscotch.

7. The students are _____ the schoolyard.

8. The target is _____ the school wall.

9. The basketball net is _____ the target and the climbing wall.

10. The hopscotch is _____ the climbing wall.

Read **and** Review

- Singular noun + **is**

  The ball **is** in the basketball net.

- Plural noun + **are**

  The balls **are** in the basket.

B Pair practice

► **Use** school objects around you to practise prepositions of position.

► **Ask** your partner where the school object is.

► **Use** the *Read and Repeat* box to help you.

Read and Repeat

Where is the pencil?

It's next to the eraser.

Good! It's your turn.

C Where are the schoolyard 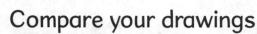 activities?

► **Read** about the schoolyard activities on the card your teacher gives you.

► **Draw** the schoolyard activities on a sheet of paper.

► **Describe** your partner's schoolyard.

D Compare your drawings

► **Compare** your drawings from Activity C with your partner.

► **Complete** the chart to say where the activities are, using prepositions of position.

► **Write** where each activity is, using full sentences.

Activity	Your name:	Your partner's name:
spider web		
monkey bars		
jungle gym		
balls		

Your name: _____

_____

_____

_____

_____

Your partner's name: _____

_____

_____

_____

_____

6 From here to there

Look at Grammar: Prepositions of movement

We use prepositions of movement to show movement to or from a place.

around the running track

up the climbing wall

down the climbing wall

into the tunnel

out of the tunnel

A Simon says

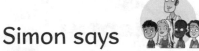

► **Play** the game with your teacher and your classmates.
► **Use** the *Look at Grammar* box to help you.

B Schoolyard obstacle course

► **Write** the correct prepositions of movement.

a) Go _____into_____ and go _____out of_____ the tunnel.

b) Climb _____ and climb _____ the spider web.

c) Jump _____ the mediation circle on one foot.

d) Run _____ the schoolyard two times.

e) Climb _____ the jungle gym and then climb _____.

C Start to finish

► **Listen** to the description of the schoolyard obstacle course from Activity B.
► **Write** the obstacles in order.

1. _____ 2. _____ 3. _____ 4. _____ 5. _____

D Your own obstacle course

► **Write** your own obstacle course with a partner.

► **Use** the *Read and Repeat* box below to help you.

Example: Run around the schoolyard two times.

1. _____

2. _____

3. _____

4. _____

5. _____

6. _____

E Out of my way!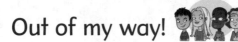

► **Mime** the actions of your obstacle course from Activity D with your partner.

► **Guess** the actions the other pair mimes.

Read and Repeat

Let's write "Run around the schoolyard two times."

Good idea!

F What can you do?

► **Read** the sentences.

► **Write** the correct prepositions of movement.

You are on the jungle gym. Your friend asks you to climb _____up_____ the climbing wall with her. You go _____ the tunnel. Oh no! It is blocked! You can't get _____ the tunnel. You want to go _____ the slide but it needs to be repaired. You decide to climb on the monkey bars and jump _____. On your way to the climbing wall, you run _____ the basket of balls and you step _____ the mediation circle. Finally, you arrive at your next activity. You climb _____ the climbing wall to see your friend. Have fun!

7 Schoolyard baseball

A It's a hit!

► **Read** the card your teacher gives you.

► **Move** around the baseball field.

► **Be** the first player to score nine points and **win** the game!

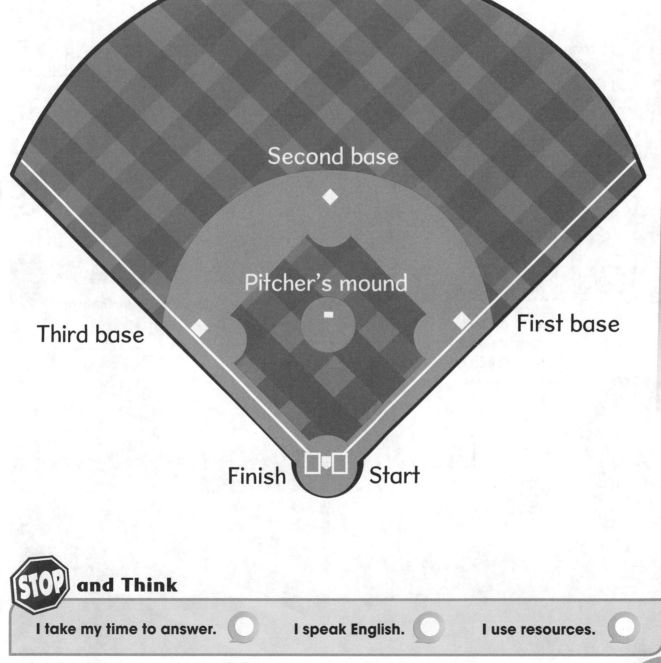

Second base

Pitcher's mound

Third base

First base

Finish   Start

STOP and Think

| I take my time to answer. | I speak English. | I use resources. |

A The new schoolyard

► **Read** the story.

► **Highlight** the **actions** in one colour, the **prepositions of position** in a different colour and the **prepositions of movement** in another colour.

The bake sale at Greenwood School is a success! The schoolyard is repaired and all the students are happy.

Look! The tunnel is not blocked anymore.
I can go into and out of the tunnel.
I can also climb on the monkey bars.

Now I can throw balls at the target!
Eddie can play basketball! He can throw
the ball into the net!

Oh! I can run around the running track!
I see the lines!

9 Link It Together

A Activities and actions

► **Choose** an activity for each of the actions.

1. throw balls _____

2. jump _____

3. climb _____

4. run _____

5. play _____

6. catch _____

B Capabilities

► **Unscramble** the words to form a question.

► **Answer** the question.

1. you • catch • ball • ? • Can • a

Can you catch a ball? _____   Yes, I can. _____

2. a • on • Can • jump • hopscotch • ? • you

_____   _____

3. Can • monkey • ? • climb • you • the • bars • on

_____   _____

4. ? • Can • throw • a • you • ball

_____   _____

5. play • ? • you • Can • basketball

_____   _____

6. around • you • run • the • ? • track • Can

_____   _____

7. you • the • ? • up • Can • climb • spider • web

_____   _____

C | Prepositions

▶ **Write** where each activity is, using prepositions of position.

▶ **Write** a preposition of movement that you can do for each activity.

1. Activity: running track

Preposition of position: _____

Preposition of movement: _____

2. Activity: tunnel

Preposition of position: _____

Preposition of movement: _____

3. Activity: hopscotch

Preposition of position: _____

Preposition of movement: _____

4. Activity: climbing wall

Preposition of position: _____

Preposition of movement: _____

D | Identification

▶ **Read** about the actions and activities.

▶ **Place** a square around the word "can."

▶ **Circle** the activities.

▶ **Highlight** the **actions** in one colour, the **prepositions of position** in a different colour and the **prepositions of movement** in another colour.

1. In my schoolyard you can climb up the climbing wall. The climbing wall is next to the basketball.

2. In my schoolyard you can play on the jungle gym. The jungle gym is behind the spider web.

3. In my schoolyard you can run around the running track. The running track is next to the mediation circle.

4. In my schoolyard you can throw and catch balls. The balls are between the spider web and the mediation circle.

5. In my schoolyard you can jump on the hopscotch. The hopscotch is in front of the climbing wall.

6. In my schoolyard you can play under the jungle gym. The jungle gym is next to the climbing wall.

10 Project: My perfect schoolyard!

A The plan

- **Choose** five activities from pages 84 and 85.

- **Add** a new activity of your choice.
  Example: trampoline

- **Draw** the activities in your perfect schoolyard.

Read and Repeat

> Let's draw a tunnel.

> I prefer monkey bars. Do you agree?

> Yes, I agree.

B The model

► **Look** at the model.

In our schoolyard you can climb up and down the climbing wall. The climbing wall is next to the target. You can throw a ball at the target. The target is between the climbing wall and the tunnel. You can go into and out of the tunnel. The tunnel is behind the spider web. You can run around the spider web. The spider web is in front of the jungle gym. You can play under the jungle gym. The jungle gym is next to the trampoline. You can jump up and down on the trampoline. It's a perfect schoolyard!

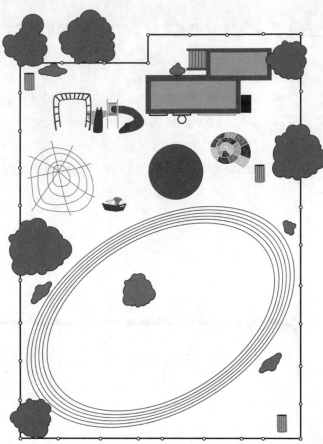

C The rough draft

► **Use** your plan from Activity A and the model from Activity B to describe your perfect schoolyard.

► **Include** the actions you can do.

► **Include** prepositions of movement.

► **Include** where each activity is, using prepositions of position.

In our schoolyard _____

_____

_____

_____

_____

_____

_____

_____

_____

_____ It's a perfect schoolyard!

D Prepare your questions

► **Use** the activities in your perfect schoolyard to write questions of capability.

Example: Can you climb up a climbing wall? Can you play on the monkey bars?

Read and Repeat

Can you play on the monkey bars?

Yes, I can.

E Interview your classmates

► **Ask** another pair of students the questions of capability from Activity D.

► In the chart below, **write** one activity they can do and one activity they can't do in your schoolyard.

► **Move** around the class and **ask** your questions of capability to other pairs.

Name	Can	Can't

Our schoolyard is perfect for:

1. _____

2. _____

Forest Adventure

lake

map

treasure

stream

GPS

compass

trail

bush

tree trunk

plant

branch

tree

rock

Let's have a treasure hunt! Plan your own treasure hunt and guide your partners to the treasure.

1 Explore!

A The forest in action

► **Look** at the illustration.

► **Repeat** the forest adventure words after your teacher.

► **Circle** the correct answers.

1. What do you see in this scene?

   a) Leo and his class run in the forest.

   b) Leo and his class get lost in the forest.

   c) Leo and his class are on a treasure hunt in the forest.

2. Where is the treasure?

   a) It is next to a rock.

   b) It is inside a tree trunk.

   c) It is on a tree branch.

B The forest and tools

► **Write** the forest adventure words from the illustration in the correct column.

Forest	Tools

C The forest and you

► **Write** forest adventure activities that you know.

_____

_____

D Exploring the forest

- ► **Read** the descriptions with your partner.
- ► **Write** the correct answer.
- ► **Use** the *Look at Words* box to help you.

L(**oo**)**k at Words**

trail

map

rock

branch

GPS

treasure

tree trunk

lake

compass

1. It is grey and hard. _____

2. It is a big part of a tree. _____

3. It shows north, south, east and west. _____

4. It is a big body of water. _____

5. It is a special object. _____

6. It is a place to walk in a forest. _____

7. It looks like a tree's arm. _____

8. It is a tool that gives the exact location of an object. _____

9. It is an illustration of a place. _____

E Class treasure hunt

- ► **Complete** the text with the forest adventure words from pages 102 and 103.

Leo and his class explore the forest to find a 1_____. Lexie looks

in a 2_____. Robin walks on the 3_____ and points

to the 4_____. Leo steps on a 5_____ and looks under

a 6_____. Ariane looks inside a 7_____. Ms. Elisabeth points

to the tools on the 8_____. She describes the tools to Eddie:

"The 9_____ is an illustration of the forest. The 10_____ shows

north, south, east and west. Use a 11_____ to find the exact location

of the treasure." The students need directions to find the treasure.

2 Directions

A The imperative

► **Repeat** the direction words after your teacher.

L👀k at Grammar: The imperative

We use the imperative form of the verb for directions.

turn right	go around	go over	stay on
turn left	go straight	go past	get off

B Tell me where to go!

► **Use** directions to guide your partner through the classroom.

► **Use** the *Look at Grammar* box to help you.

Go straight to the chair. Turn left. Go past the teacher's desk.

STOP and Think

I cooperate. ⬤   I practise. ⬤   I use what I know. ⬤

Map

▶ **Look** carefully at the map.

▶ **Use** the map for the activities on page 107.

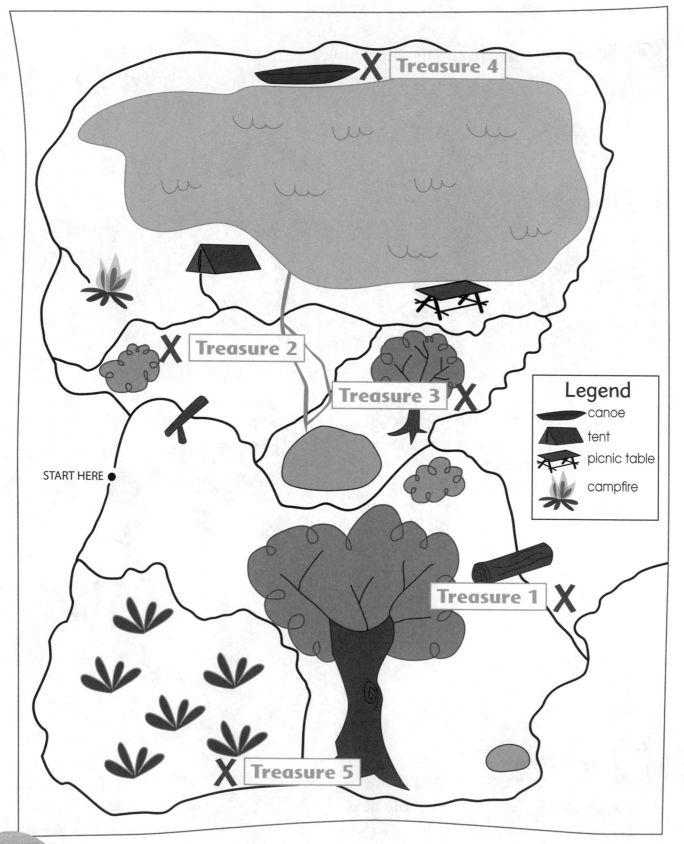

D Treasure!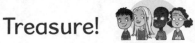

► **Take turns** reading the clues on the cards your teacher gives you.

► **Look** at the map on page 106.

► **Write** the number of the treasure you find.

1. Treasure ☐ **3.** Treasure ☐

2. Treasure ☐ **4.** Treasure ☐

I think the answer is Treasure 2.

I agree!

E Be my forest guide

► **Write** directions to get from one place in the forest to another.

► **Read** your directions to a partner.

► **Use** the map on page 106 and the *Look at Grammar* box on page 105 to help you.

1. Start at the big rock. Go straight. Turn right at the lake. _____

Where are you? at the picnic table _____

2. _____

Where are you? _____

3. _____

Where are you? _____

4. _____

Where are you? _____

5. _____

Where are you? _____

F Map it

► **Listen** to the directions.

► **Look** at the map on page 106.

► **Write** where the directions take you.

1. _____ **3.** _____

2. _____ **4.** _____

3 Asking questions

Lk at Grammar: Question words

We use question words to ask about specific information.

Who? a person
> **Who** is on a treasure hunt?
> Lexie.

Where? a place
> **Where** is the treasure?
> In the tree trunk.

What? an object, an animal, an action
> **What** does Ariane see?
> A treasure.

How? a manner
> **How** do they find the treasure?
> With a GPS.

When? a time
> **When** do they go on a treasure hunt?
> In the summer.

A Where do they go?

► **Write** the words under the correct question word.

► **Use** the *Look at Grammar* box to help you.

- Ms. Elisabeth
- go past the stream
- June
- under a rock
- go over the tree branch

- Robin
- summer
- next to a bush
- bush
- with a compass

- after school
- plant
- in the forest
- branch
- Eddie

Who?	What?	When?	Where?	How?
		June		

B Which question word?

► **Write** the correct question words.

► **Use** the *Look at Grammar* box on page 108 to help you.

1. <u>When</u> is the last day of school? <u>June 22</u>.

2. _____ is your partner? My partner is <u>Robin</u>.

3. _____ is the treasure? The treasure is <u>under</u> the rock.

4. _____ is your treasure? My treasure is a <u>book</u>.

5. _____ do you spell lake? L – A – K – E.

6. _____ is summer? In one <u>month</u>!

7. _____ is this adventure tool? It's a <u>compass</u>.

8. _____ is the big rock? It is <u>next to</u> the stream.

9. _____ do you get to the big tree? <u>Stay on</u> the trail.

C Dominoes

► **Listen** to your teacher and **play** the game.

► **Be** the first player to play all your dominoes and **win** the game!

Read and Repeat

I have a domino with "Who?" It goes with "Robin." It's your turn.

I don't have a domino that matches "Under a plant." I have to pick a card.

| When? | Robin | Who? | Under a plant. |

| July | What? |

4 Story time

A Prepare to read

▶ **Skim** the story and **answer** the questions.

1. What is the title of the story? _____

2. Predict what the story is about. Circle your answer.

   a) a treasure hunt

   b) a picnic in the forest

   c) a walk in the forest

3. Name two forest tools you need for this type of activity.

_____   _____

L⦿⦿k at Words

geocache: a box with a logbook and a treasure inside

logbook: a book to write information

coordinates: numbers that show the exact location of an object

B Story: Geocaching: A Different Kind of Treasure Hunt

▶ **Listen** to the story and **read** along.

Geocaching is an outdoor treasure hunt activity for

everybody. The goal of geocaching is to find a **geocache** .

A geocache is a plastic box where you can find treasures like toys, books and more.

 When you find the geocache, you take the treasure out and replace it with

a treasure of your own. In the geocache, there is also a **logbook**. It is very

important to complete the logbook with your name and the date. A geocache can be in

a forest, in a park, in a city or anywhere! There are probably many geocaches

close to you right now!

To find a geocache, you need a GPS . The GPS gives you the **coordinates**

to find the geocache.

To do the activity, you have to follow seven steps.

Before the activity

1. Go to a geocaching website with your parents.

2. Choose a geocache from the list.

3. Enter the coordinates of the geocache into your GPS.

During the activity

4. Use your GPS to find the geocache.

5. When you find the geocache, you replace the treasure with a treasure of your own.

6. Sign the logbook and return the geocache to its original location.

After the activity

7. Share your geocaching stories and photos online.

Geocaching is a great way to end the school year! Go outside with your classmates and have fun!

Remember!

✓ Go geocaching with an adult.
✓ Work in pairs.
✓ Tell someone where you are going.
✓ Bring water.

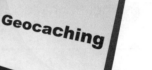

C Show you understand

► **Scan** the story to find the answers.

1. Circle the action you do in geocaching but not on a treasure hunt.

   a) Follow directions.

   b) Find a treasure.

   c) Replace the treasure with one of your own.

2. Place the geocaching steps in order.

Complete the logbook. ☐   Choose a geocache. ☐

Share your story online. ☐   Find the geocache. ☐

3. Where can you find a geocache?

_____

4. What do you find in a geocache?

_____

5. When do you complete the logbook?

_____

6. Name two things you have to remember when you go geocaching.

_____

7. Do you want to go geocaching this summer? If yes, with who?

I would like to go with _____

Geocaching

🛑 **and Think**

| I predict. ◯ | I pay attention. ◯ | I don't understand everything and that's okay. ◯ |

5 Making plans

L👀k at Grammar: The future

We use *will* to talk about the future.

Singular	Plural	
I will	We will	The main verb stays in the infinitive form.
You will	You will	They **will camp** in the forest.
He/She/It will	They will	The tools **will be** on the picnic table.

A A future adventure

► **Highlight** the verbs.

► **Write** the sentences in the future.

► **Use** the *Look at Grammar* box to help you.

Now	Next summer
1. I walk in the forest.	I will walk in the forest.
2. He camps.	_____
3. We take pictures of animals.	_____
4. You look for animal tracks.	_____
5. They have a picnic.	_____
6. It is warm.	_____
7. She hunts for a treasure.	_____
8. You find treasures.	_____

B On my treasure hunt, I will see...

► **Test** your memory.

► **Add** a forest word or an adventure tool when it's your turn.

► **Use** the *Read and Repeat* box to help you.

Read **and** Repeat

On my treasure hunt, I will see a tree.

On my treasure hunt, I will see a tree and a compass.

C Guessing game

► **Highlight** your choice for each number.
► **Guess** what your partner will do.
► **Use** the *Read and Repeat* box to help you.

On my treasure hunt . . .

1. I will go into the forest with **a friend** /
my parents.

2. I will bring **a map** / **a compass** / **a GPS**.

3. I will put my treasure in **a plastic box** / **a bag**.

4. I will use **a book** / **a toy** as my treasure.

5. I will hide my treasure **in a tree trunk** / **next to the lake** / **under a rock**.

6. I will go **in June** / **in July** / **in August**.

7. I will share **my story** / **my pictures** / **my treasure** with my friends.

8. I will remember to **work in pairs** / **tell someone where we will go** / **bring water**.

D Find someone who...

► **Write** your choices from Activity C in the chart below.
► **Find** a classmate who has the same choice as you.
► **Write** the classmate's name in the chart.

Me	A classmate
Example: I will go into the forest with my parents.	Ariane
1.	
2.	
3.	
4.	
5.	
6.	
7.	
8.	

6 Learn and play

A Reader's theatre

► **Listen** to the play and **read** along.
► **Choose** a role and **read** your part.
► **Decide** what the treasure is.
► **Practise** with your teammates.

Look at Words

hurry: do something rapidly

turn over: place something with the bottom on the top

The Greenwood Treasure Hunt

Narrator It is an exciting day for the students of Greenwood School. They are on a treasure hunt in the forest. Who will find the treasure first?

Leo This is a fun activity to end the school year!

Eddie Yes! You and I will find the treasure first!

Narrator In another part of the forest, Lexie, Ariane and Robin also try to find the treasure.

Lexie I hope we find the treasure!

Robin Yes! The treasure is next to the lake. Where are we now?

Narrator The students stop and hear the sound of water. It's a stream! Ariane looks at the map. She points to the map.

Ariane Look! We are here!

Narrator Eddie and Leo walk on a trail. They look at Ms. Elisabeth's directions.

Eddie The directions say, "Turn right on the trail. Go straight and go past the stream."

Leo Let's continue!

Narrator Suddenly, Leo steps on a branch. It goes "CRACK!"

Lexie What is that noise?

Robin It's Leo and Eddie! Come on, let's **hurry**!

Ariane We have to get off the trail and turn left at the rock.

Narrator Eddie uses Ms. Elisabeth's directions to find the lake. Leo and Eddie catch up to Lexie, Robin and Ariane. They all run to the lake. They get there at the same time. They look for the treasure.

Lexie I think the treasure is under the canoe! It will be difficult to **turn** it **over**!

Leo We can help you! Let's all work together!

Narrator With great teamwork, the friends turn over the canoe. The treasure is there!

It's a _____ !

7 Link It Together

A Sounds like an adventure!

► **Listen** to the descriptions of the forest words and the adventure tools.

► **Write** the correct words.

1. _____
2. _____
3. _____
4. _____
5. _____
6. _____
7. _____

8. _____
9. _____
10. _____
11. _____
12. _____
13. _____
14. _____

B Directions: To the treasure!

► **Read** the text.

► **Look** at the direction symbols.

► **Write** the correct directions.

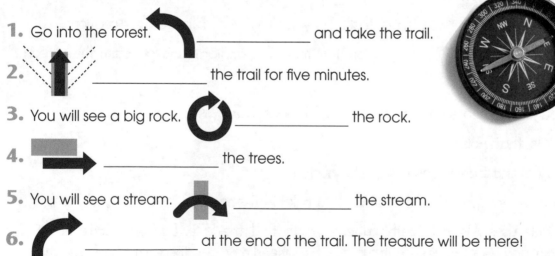

1. Go into the forest. _____ and take the trail.

2. _____ the trail for five minutes.

3. You will see a big rock. _____ the rock.

4. _____ the trees.

5. You will see a stream. _____ the stream.

6. _____ at the end of the trail. The treasure will be there!

© 2015, Les Éditions CEC, inc. • **Reproduction prohibited**

C · What will they do?

- ► **Look** at the word bank.
- ► **Choose** the correct activity for each person.
- ► **Write** your sentences in the future.

eat in the forest	play hide-and-seek	run in the forest	pick up rocks
camp in a tent	go for a canoe ride	fish	cook marshmallows

1. Lexie likes to run.   She will run in the forest. _____

2. Leo likes to camp.   _____

3. Robin and Lexie like to eat marshmallows. _____

4. Eddie and I like to hide.   _____

5. I like to be on the lake.   _____

6. Ariane and Eddie collect rocks.   _____

7. Lexie likes to fish with her father. _____

8. The friends like picnic lunches.   _____

D · Geocaching!

- ► **Write** the correct question word.

1. _____ is the activity to end the school year? Geocaching.

2. _____ will come with us? Our teacher and our classmates.

3. _____ will we go? On June 5.

4. _____ adventure tools will we bring? A GPS, a compass and a map.

5. _____ will we go? In the forest.

6. _____ will we find the geocache? We will follow directions.

7. _____ is the best time to go geocaching? In summer.

8. _____ will find the treasure? I will!

STOP and Think

| I use resources. ◯ | I ask for help or clarification. ◯ | I take risks. ◯ |

8 Project: Plan your own treasure hunt

A The plan

▶ **Read** the questions.

▶ **Share** your ideas with your partner.

▶ **Take** notes on the lines.

1. Who will be your partner?

_____

2. What will you use as your treasure?

_____

3. Where will you hide your treasure?

_____

4. When will you hide your treasure?

_____

5. What tools will you need?

_____

6. What will your forest look like? Draw a small sketch of your forest on a piece of paper or use the map on page 106. Draw an X for your treasure.

7. How will we find your treasure? Write the directions.

_____

_____

_____

B The model

▶ **Look** at the model.

Ariane will be my partner. We will use a book as our treasure. We will hide our treasure in a tree trunk. We will hide our treasure on Saturday. We will need a compass and a map.

Here are the directions to find our treasure. Start at the rock. Turn left on the trail. Walk past the bush and get off the trail. Go over the tree trunk and turn right at the big tree. Can you find our treasure?

C The rough draft

► **Use** your plan from Activity A and the model from Activity B to write your treasure hunt plan.

_____

_____

_____

_____

_____

_____

_____

_____

_____

_____

D The presentation

► **Locate** the treasure on another pair's map.

► **Tell** them how you get there (the directions).

► **Guess** what their treasure is.

Resources

Verbs

The verb *to be*

Simple present

	Affirmative	Negative
I	am	am not
You	are	are not
He/She/It	is	is not
We	are	are not
You	are	are not
They	are	are not

Future

	Affirmative	Negative
I	will be	will not be
You	will be	will not be
He/She/It	will be	will not be
We	will be	will not be
You	will be	will not be
They	will be	will not be

Imperative

Be quiet.   **Do not be** late.

The verb *to have*

Simple present

	Affirmative	Negative
I	have	do not have
You	have	do not have
He/She/It	has	does not have
We	have	do not have
You	have	do not have
They	have	do not have

Future

	Affirmative	Negative
I	will have	will not have
You	will have	will not have
He/She/It	will have	will not have
We	will have	will not have
You	will have	will not have
They	will have	will not have

Imperative

Have an apple.   **Do not have** a cookie.

Regular verbs

Simple present

	Affirmative	Negative
I	talk	do not talk
You	talk	do not talk
He/She/It	talks	does not talk
We	talk	do not talk
You	talk	do not talk
They	talk	do not talk

Future

	Affirmative	Negative
I	will talk	will not talk
You	will talk	will not talk
He/She/It	will talk	will not talk
We	will talk	will not talk
You	will talk	will not talk
They	will talk	will not talk

Imperative

Talk to your partner   **Do not talk** in the hallway.

Question words

Who?	a person	**Who** is at the potluck?
What?	an object, an animal, an action	**What** are you eating?
When?	a time	**When** are we going?
Where?	a place	**Where** is it?
How?	a manner	**How** will we get there?

L👀k at Grammar

Pronouns

Singular	I	you	he	she	it

| Plural | we | you | they |

Asking questions in the present

Preferences

Do you like painting?   Yes, I do.

Do you like basketball?   No, I do not. / No, I don't.

Other possibilities with *do*

Do you have hockey skates?   Yes, I do.

Where?

Where is the teacher?   She is in the classroom.

Where are the students?   They are in the cafeteria.

Prepositions of place

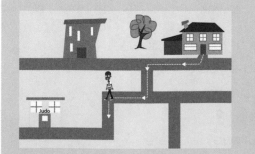

Eddie goes **to** the judo studio on Fridays.

Eddie is **at** the judo studio.

Prepositions of time

Prepositions	Time categories	Examples
at	time	I have judo **at** <u>6:00</u>.
on	day	I have judo **on** <u>Wednesday</u>.
	date	I have judo **on** <u>January 8</u>.
in	part of day	I have judo **in** <u>the afternoon</u>.
	month	I have judo **in** <u>January</u>.
	season	I have judo **in** <u>winter</u>.

Possessive adjectives

Singular: my · your · his · her · its

Plural: our · your · their

Prepositions of position

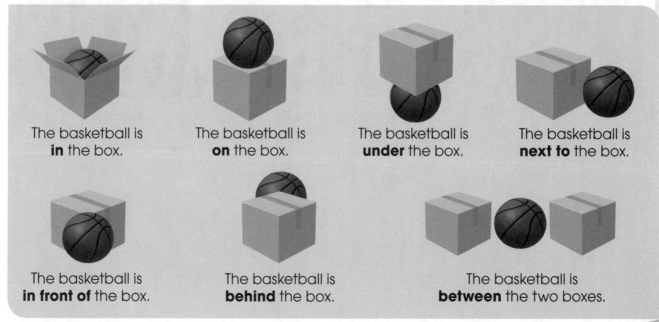

The basketball is **in** the box.

The basketball is **on** the box.

The basketball is **under** the box.

The basketball is **next to** the box.

The basketball is **in front of** the box.

The basketball is **behind** the box.

The basketball is **between** the two boxes.

Describing things

Singular
There is beef in the enchiladas.
There is vegetable soup on the table.

Plural
There are eggs in the cake.
There are cookies on the table.

Capabilities

Question	Affirmative	Negative
Can you catch?	Yes, I **can**.	No, I **cannot**. / No, I **can't**.
Can she jump?	Yes, she **can**.	No, she **cannot**. / No, she **can't**.
Can he throw?	Yes, he **can**.	No, he **cannot**. / No, he **can't**.

Prepositions of movement

around the running track

up the climbing wall

down the climbing wall

into the tunnel

out of the tunnel

STOP and Think

Comprehension strategies

I predict.

I think it's about a party.

I pay attention.

I infer.

It's a red fruit. Maybe it's an apple.

I scan the story to find the answers.

Communication strategies

I practise.

My name is Leo.
My name is Leo.

I speak English.

My name is Leo.

I use what I know.

I take risks.

Problem-solving strategies

I use resources.

I ask for help or clarification.

I cooperate.

I don't understand everything and that's okay.

Photo credits